Praise for *Read Outside Your Bubble*

"Everyone needs a copy of *Read Outside Your Bubble* in their classroom and at home libraries! It is a transformative, crucial read about the importance of reading inclusive books."

—**Kaitlin Johnstone**, cofounder, Kind Cotton

"In *Read Outside Your Bubble*, Nita Creekmore calls educators to bring diverse voices into their classrooms, building spaces of trust, connection, and transformation. Through her LEAP framework and practical classroom insights, Nita guides teachers on a courageous path, showing how inclusive texts deepen relationships, inspire greater learning, and empower us to meet today's challenges with purpose and intention."

—**Lori Cohen**, coauthor of *The PD Book: 7 Habits That Transform Professional Development*

"Nita Creekmore's *Read Outside Your Bubble* inspired me to rethink how I approach reading and teaching. Her blend of personal stories and practical strategies makes stepping outside our familiar boundaries both accessible and necessary. This book is essential for anyone seeking to foster empathy and inclusivity through literature!"

—**LaNesha Tabb**, author, speaker, and founder of Reimagine Writing

"Nita's LEAP framework is everything a teacher needs to build an inclusive and empathetic literacy curriculum that truly resonates with students. As an instructional coach, this is my go-to resource for working with teachers as we build impactful classrooms that engage students beyond their 'bubbles' and foster a love for diverse perspectives. The framework goes beyond academics; it's a transformative approach that prepares students for a more inclusive world by inspiring compassion, critical thinking, and meaningful impact. Nita's research-backed steps make it easy for educators to create classrooms that leave a lasting, positive impression on students' lives."

—**Nicole S. Turner**, author and CEO of Simply Instructional Coaching

"*Read Outside Your Bubble* is a wonderful resource on the importance of diverse perspectives in the books that we read to our students. This book provides educators, instructional facilitators and administrators with a deep understanding of how varied voices can enrich classroom discussions and foster empathy. Nita shares her immense knowledge as an educator, parent, and instructional coach on the importance of incorporating inclusive books in order to learn more about our beautifully diverse world."

—**Jenny LaRocque,** educator and author

"Nita Creekmore has written a book that I will be gifting to every educator I can. It is not just a powerful book but a necessary one. The impact and gift of literacy cannot go understated and Nita has perfectly encapsulated not only the importance of books but the real value in consuming a wide variety and how much it can change a life. I can't praise this book enough! I have sticky notes all over it!"

—**Todd Nesloney,** director of Culture and Strategic Leadership at the Texas Elementary Principals and Supervisors Association (TEPSA)

"*Read Outside Your Bubble* is a compelling dive into the world of lesser-chosen reads, encouraging readers to step outside their comfort zones and open themselves to a myriad of books."

—**Silvana Spence,** founder of the STEAM SQUAD LLC and author of *Bella the Scientist Goes to Outer Space*

Read Outside Your Bubble

Read Outside Your Bubble

Expand Your Bookshelf, Expand Your World

Nita Creekmore

JB JOSSEY-BASS™
A Wiley Brand

Jossey-Bass, a Wiley imprint

Published by John Wiley & Sons, Inc., Hoboken, New Jersey.
Published simultaneously in Canada.

For general information on our other products and services, please contact our Customer Care Department within the United States at (800) 762-2974, outside the United States at (317) 572-3993. For product technical support, you can find answers to frequently asked questions or reach us via live chat at https://support.wiley.com.

If you believe you've found a mistake in this book, please bring it to our attention by emailing our reader support team at wileysupport@wiley.com with the subject line "Possible Book Errata Submission."

Wiley also publishes its books in a variety of electronic formats. Some content that appears in print may not be available in electronic formats. For more information about Wiley products, visit our web site at www.wiley.com.

Library of Congress Cataloging-in-Publication Data is Available:

ISBN 9781394244638 (Paperback)
ISBN 9781394244645 (ePub)
ISBN 9781394244652 (ePDF)

Cover Design: Wiley
Cover Images: © retouchman/Getty Images, © malerapaso/Getty Images

SKY10096980_012325

To my loving husband, Michael, and our amazing children, Bryson, Aspen, Simone, and Eva—my entire family. Your love and support have been my guiding light. You are the reason the search for diverse stories that reflect mirrors, windows and sliding glass doors was ignited. May you continue to expand your bubbles and embrace the richness of our world, making it a more compassionate and human place for all.

To my mother who introduced mirror books to me at a young age. Thank you for all your unconditional love and support.

To my students past, present, and future I hope you use inclusive books to change the world one drop at a time.

To my dearest yaya sisters—your support has always meant the world to me. Thank you for always tellling me to shine bright. Love you both. #lovetranscends

Contents

Contents

Foreword by Charnaie Gordon

There may come a time in life when you realize your world feels smaller than it should. Maybe it's a quiet realization when you're scrolling through social media and see conversations you've never had. Or perhaps it's a sharp jolt when someone shares a perspective that challenges everything you thought you knew. Either way, that's your bubble tapping you on the shoulder. It's a reminder that your life, your choices, and your reading habits are all shaped by the limits of what you've allowed in and what you've intentionally or unintentionally kept out.

I remember the first time I realized I had been living inside my own bubble. It wasn't intentional; it's just what happens when you lean into what feels familiar and safe. My bookshelf, my friends, my worldview—they all reflected what I already knew and believed. But one day, while in college, I began reading more books by authors of color. The stories I read shook me. They forced me to sit with discomfort, beauty, and truths that were outside of my lived experience. I read books that were mirrors, windows, and doors all at once. That's the power of reading.

Nita Creekmore captures this idea perfectly in *Read Outside Your Bubble*. With her warmth, insight, and ability to challenge without judgment, she invites readers to reconsider not just what we read but how we live. This book gently guides you toward a richer, fuller way of being in the world through relationships, reading, and intentional growth.

The beauty of this book lies in its practicality. You won't just be told to "read more inclusively" and left to figure it out on your own. Instead, Nita introduces her LEAP framework—Learning, Equity, Access, and Purpose—a roadmap for making inclusive reading part of your everyday life. She'll help you find books that reflect the world's diversity and teach you how to use them in ways that deepen understanding, spark curiosity, and transform conversations.

I recommend this book for educators, librarians, parents, or anyone who wants to expand their bookshelf and their world. It's for those who've realized they've been standing still while the world moves forward. It's for the curious souls who are ready to push past comfort and into growth. And yes, it's for the skeptics who might think, "Does this really matter?" (Spoiler: It absolutely does!)

I love how Nita challenges us to think about books as more than stories. They're tools for empathy, change, and connection. Each chapter builds on this idea, showing us how books can be mirrors that reflect our experiences, windows into other worlds, and sliding-glass doors that invite us to step outside ourselves. Through her words, you'll see how reading outside your bubble can help you build relationships, dismantle biases, and see the world and yourself more clearly.

The chapter on banned books hit me the hardest. Nita flips the script, reframing these often controversial stories as *VIBs*: Very Important Books. These are the stories someone doesn't want you to read, which makes them all the more essential. It's a powerful reminder that every time we choose to read outside our bubbles, we're making a statement: we refuse to be closed off. We refuse to be stuck. We choose growth, connection, and understanding.

So here's my challenge to you: let this book be your invitation to POP YOUR BUBBLE! Start with curiosity. Let Nita's wisdom guide you as you fill your bookshelves and your heart with stories that challenge, inspire, and expand you.

My Why

As a child I have always looked for someone who looked like me in the pages of the books that I read. It began when I was little, and the desire has not gone away. I've always looked for myself or someone who looks like me in movies, TV shows, schools, and my places of work. Representation in the areas of my life matters. It has always mattered to me and still does even as an adult.

Books are no different. When I was a child in elementary school, there weren't many books that had covers with someone of color displayed on the cover and definitely not as the protagonist in the story. As a child, it was something I craved. It was something I needed. I wanted to read books that represented Black girls like me.

Growing up, my family instilled in me a great deal of self-worth and always made me feel seen, valued, and enough—even when the world was saying otherwise. My family was my rock when I had difficult times in school making friends or when I was struggling to read. They were always there to remind me of my genius.

Still, in kindergarten through fourth grade I felt unseen. In my elementary years, I was often one of the only Black students in my classrooms. Up until fifth grade I hadn't had one Black teacher. I think that this has a huge effect on how I showed up in school and how much I felt seen and valued. For example, my parents would push me and have high expectations for me as a student, but when I got into the school building, I was often in a space where as long as I was doing enough, it was okay. But inherently it was not okay. I needed my teachers to see me—really see me—and push me to my potential. I needed them to have representation in their classrooms, in the curriculum they taught, and in the stories they read—the stories I read. I needed them to give me the tools so that I could show my genius. Needless to say, I pushed through regardless of this lack of representation.

When I decided to become an educator in 1997, a goal of mine was to ensure that all students felt seen, valued, and heard in my classroom. I wanted them to feel this in how I treated them, in the walls of my classroom, and in the curriculum. I wanted them to feel they were a part of our community, and one way to do that was to make sure they were represented in all areas of our learning community, even in the books they picked up from the shelves.

When students feel valued, seen, and heard in their classroom community, they not only learn at higher levels, but they feel emotionally and psychologically safe in the classroom. They connect with their teachers and their classmates, and a learning community is built. I did not need to dig into research on that theory because I *am* the research. I know it because I have lived it. I know it because I have felt it. I know it because I have built relationships with students where they have shared with me about past experiences in classrooms where they felt less than seen and valued. I know it because it's my truth. When students can see themselves and others that look like them in the books that they read and the curriculum they are taught, they will soar to great heights.

Don't just go find the research—be the research. I invite you to take the step, the plunge, and see just how much your students soar by ensuring that they see themselves in books, in curriculum, and in your learning environment. They should see others as well so that their bubbles are expanded, which expands their world.

What Does the Title of This Book Mean?

Reading outside of your bubble is a phrase I created and began hashtagging on my @loveteachbless Instagram page. I have always shared inclusive and diverse books with my own children, with my students in my classroom, and with students in other classrooms. But I also began sharing inclusive books on my social media page. I shared these books because I wanted to open other folks' worlds to the importance of diverse literature. I wanted to be able to also support Black, Indigenous, and People of Color (BIPOC) authors and illustrators.

I wanted to share their work and their art. When I shared their inclusive texts, I began using the #readoutsideyourbubble hashtag because I realized that so many folks stay comfortable in their own bubbles, learning about themselves, reading about themselves, and reading about their own communities and their own experiences. There is power in that, especially if you're reading and learning about your own bubble that is not offered in schools. In other words, if you are learning more about yourself, your culture, your lineage, or your identity that isn't taught in schools, reading inside your bubble is essential. I believe that it is important to start within your own bubble. Taking time to learn about who you are, where you came from, your history, and your ancestors is essential. It is pertinent to know who you are and digging into your identity and its intersections is a great place to begin.

I also believe that we cannot just stay inside our bubbles. Learning about ourselves is a continuous journey, but I believe we can do both simultaneously. We must take time to learn about others outside of our bubbles. The use of inclusive books is a great place to begin, especially in schools. Expanding our bubbles makes us better humans. Once we realize and accept that we are different, and our differences should be honored and celebrated, we can begin to ignite change. We are different, beautiful, and interconnected.

Once we come together in community, our world will be stronger, better, and more humane. Without community, freedom is harder to attain. We are threaded together. That is what reading outside our bubbles is about. Reading outside our bubbles is reading and teaching with inclusive books at the center in culturally responsive ways. Inclusive books, or diverse literature, are books that are welcoming to all readers that also include a variety of perspectives and experiences. They can help readers see themselves and others in the pages of a book. Inclusive books can help break down barriers, release stereotypes, unlearn biases, and increase perspective-taking. Inclusive books can also help readers learn about different communities, races, cultures, genders, lives, and orientation, and can help readers to develop understanding, empathy, and compassion. That is the essence of reading outside your bubble because when you do so, you expand your bookshelf, and you expand your world in the process.

Why I Wrote This Book

I did not decide to become a teacher just to teach. I love teaching, yes, but I became a teacher to change the world. As naive as that may sound to some, it's the truth. I knew that by teaching that I could help to change the world one student at a time by the connections I made, the relationships I cultivated, and the lessons that I taught them. I decided to write this book as a pathway to continue fulfilling that—a pathway to changing the world.

This book, *Reading Outside Your Bubble,* is about reading and learning about ourselves and reading and learning about others who may look like us. It is about reading and learning about those who may not look like us. I wrote this book for educators and families to realize why reading outside your bubble is so powerful and why teaching inside and outside your bubble can be powerful too. Reading outside your bubble can change the world—I believe that, and I have hope in that. I have written this book to include pathways to take to read and learn outside of your own bubbles as educators and to teach students to read and learn outside their bubbles as well. I wrote this book for folks who are doing this work but also for folks that want to do more and may not know where to begin. This book will help you bring inclusive and diverse literature into classrooms, but to not just end there. I want this book to also be a bridge that can be used to cultivate and foster the relationships with students and teachers, to cultivate active readers, and to increase reading engagement of our students.

The Pathway

I created the LEAP framework that anyone can use to help to guide themselves through the process of truly cultivating a learning environment that immerses inclusive texts in their curriculum. If you are a homeschool parent/guardian, you can do the same. This framework stands for Learning, Equity, Accessibility, and Purposeful and professional learning. It helps to guide educators into learning and expanding your bubbles for yourselves and our students, how to make reading outside your bubbles equitable and accessible to all, and how to cultivate community and alignment in the learning environment.

When students read outside their bubbles through mirrors, windows and sliding-glass doors, metaphors used by the great Dr. Rudine Sims Bishop, they are engulfing themselves in text in a way that increases self-acceptance, acceptance of others, connection, and engagement. This aids in creating lifelong readers and learners. Students are more open to learning, and they learn at great heights. They can showcase their genius because they have read about others who came before them that have showcased theirs unapologetically.

Knowing the importance of reading outside our bubbles is a critical step to being able to do this work. Rooting in that purpose is what will be our guide in ensuring that we continue and won't falter. Expanding our world to make it better is life's work. It is what we are called to do.

What You Will Find in This Book

Reading Outside Your Bubble is a book that not only encourages you to read inclusive and diverse books but to take that learning as an educator into your learning environments to reach and teach all students. We want all students to read inside and outside their bubbles to learn more about themselves and others to help to cultivate a more inclusive world—a world where compassion, empathy, and love are increased. Throughout each chapter in this book, you will find what it takes foundationally to read outside your bubble, you will learn about the different stages of the LEAP framework, and you will learn about ways to navigate book bans as an educator in schools. As you read each of these chapters, I invite you to identify growth areas as well as reflect on ways you can step into action. This book is for all of us—either as a reminder, a push, or an ignition to begin doing this work for ourselves, for our students, and for our learning communities.

Chapter 1, What Is a Bubble?

In Chapter 1, I discuss what a "bubble" is and what it means when I say "read outside your bubble." You will learn the importance of being a learner yourself in doing this work. You will reflect on how being a learner is important to growing your student's learning, their reading, their engagement, and their love of learning. I emphasize in this chapter that educators must be willing to do the work of reading and learning outside their bubbles as well as expanding the bubbles of their students in their learning communities.

Chapter 2, Expand Your Relationship Bubble: Relationships and Reading

In Chapter 2, I emphasize just how important it is to build relationships in your classroom. As an educator, before the teaching and learning happens, you must ensure that all our students feel seen, valued, and heard. You must take time to build relationships and cultivate a healthy, safe classroom community for this to happen. This chapter takes you through a variety of ways that we, as educators, can build relationships with our students and ways to cultivate students' healthy relationship to reading and learning.

Chapter 3, The LEAP Framework for Inclusive Texts

In Chapter 3, the LEAP framework is broken down into its four sections—Learning, Equitability, Accessibility, and Purposeful and professional learning. The purpose behind the LEAP framework is discussed in this chapter.

This chapter emphasizes the importance of each of the four areas of the framework ensuring that inclusivity permeates within your room learning community in equitable and accessible ways. In this chapter, I explain the importance of this framework for yourself, your students, and your learning community.

Chapter 4, Learning: Seeing Mirrors with Inclusive Text

In Chapter 4, you will read about the importance of representation in reading and learning in classrooms using Dr. Rudine Bishop's mirror analogy for students to feel seen, heard, and valued. In this chapter, you will read examples of the use of inclusive literature being integrated within the learning and how that can increase the feeling of inclusiveness, belonging, and psychological safety in your learning environment. I share examples through my experiences with seeing mirrors through inclusive texts and how I have used mirrors in my classroom as well.

Chapter 5, Learning: Opening Windows with Inclusive Text

In Chapter 5, you will learn how to open windows for students to learn and see people who may not look, sound, believe, or love like them. You will also learn how to celebrate, honor, and respect their stories. You will identify and tap into window reading strategies to use in your classrooms for this to come alive. I share stories through my experience of opening windows for students. Using mirrors, this chapter will share strategies on how this can be captured in your classrooms.

Chapter 6, Learning: Gliding Through Sliding Glass Doors with Inclusive Text

In Chapter 6, I discuss what it looks and sounds like when a reader enters the world of people who may be different from them and yet still beautiful using reading outside their bubbles. I will dive into what it really means to read using sliding-glass doors and how that piece often gets missed while reading. The learning and celebration of differences is highlighted again in this chapter. There are also sliding-glass door strategies on how to cultivate this in your learning spaces.

Chapter 7, Equitable: Integrating Inclusive Texts in Equitable Ways

In Chapter 7, you will read about various ways to make reading outside your bubble equitable for all students in the learning environment. You will receive strategies on how to make learning equitable and ways to keep your equitable lens on at all times. Equity is important when reading outside your bubble and expanding that reading into the curriculum. You will receive strategies on how to do this work intentionally in this chapter.

Chapter 8, Access: Getting Inclusive Texts in Everyone's Hands

In Chapter 8, we will discuss the importance of accessibility. A variety of strategies are highlighted to make inclusive texts accessible for educators and students. You will also read about how to not only make the texts accessible but to also make the learning using inclusive text accessible to students.

Chapter 9, Purposeful and Professional Learning: Building Skill and Routine to Transform

In Chapter 9, we discuss the importance of professional development and doing this work intentionally with integrity and with and alongside others. Professional learning should be ongoing, and this chapter shows ways to provide professional learning, steps to take, and how to continue professional learning.

Chapter 10, Banned Books = VIBs (Very Important Books)

In Chapter 10, I discuss what to do if banned books are a problem in your learning community. I offer a reframe in this chapter that has served me well. You will learn why I call banned books Very Important Books (VIBs). I share stories of others who have been subject to book bans and what they have done to continue to advocate for the freedom to read. This chapter also highlights the importance of being knowledgeable about the policies in the learning communities that you teach and keeping up-to-date with new policies that may arise. I also give tips to help navigate teaching with these very important books in intentional ways.

This work begins with us. Reading this book is a great way to begin the work of reading outside your bubble. This book is an offering to you and to your students. I am thankful that you have purchased this book. I am grateful it is in your hands and hope that you have invited others to do this learning and growing alongside you. This book is an invitation, and there may be times as you read that you may align with the ideas in it and times when you may disagree. As you take time to read and learn throughout this book, at the end of each chapter there is an invitation to reflect. I suggest you allow yourself the gift of pause and reflection. I'm excited for your learning journey. Let's do this good work of reading outside our bubbles together in community.

Let's Reflect

1. Why did you decide to read this book?
2. What does the title of this book, *Read Outside Your Bubble: Expand Your Bookshelf, Expand Your World*, mean to you?
3. What do you think the title of this book, *Read Outside Your Bubble: Expand Your Bookshelf, Expand Your World*, means to the students you serve?
4. What do you hope to get from this book by the time you finish it?

Chapter 1
What Is a Bubble?

Bubble

Bubbles are translucent globules that are usually hollow and light. When thinking about the word *globules*, the word that immediately comes up for me is globe. A globe is a spherical, rounded object. If you begin to mesh the two together to find connection, you can compare the hollow, translucent bubble to a globe or a world, filled with spaces, places, and diverse people. The individual bubble is hollow and translucent; however, when it becomes filled like a globe with learning and connections to self and others, it is no longer hollow. However, that bubble can still float. It gives the appearance of being light in weight because gravity is holding the globe, or the world, in place. When expanded, the bubble can be filled with light and beauty just like the world—the globe.

When I thought about the best way to explain what the bubble actually is as it relates to reading outside your bubble, I began thinking about how a bubble for a person is formed. I thought about what makes a person stay enclosed in their perspective bubble and what would intrigue a person to expand outside of their bubble to see—not only a translucent bubble but a bubble expanded filled with color, diversity, and beauty.

The bubble for a person is a space where they begin to grow and learn about themselves through knowledge, experiences, and their environment. As a person continues to grow and learn about themselves, they access knowledge they have learned either directly or indirectly. They gain experiences by moving through life within their bubbles. A person also reads and learns in their bubble because of the environment that surrounds them and the environment they are accustomed to. The bubble continues to form, and it creates a translucent globule around them.

Learning about who you are in your bubble and remaining in your bubble are not bad things. In fact, your bubble is a great place to begin knowing yourself, your identity, and the core of who you are, and, as life continues, learning about yourself will continue. But as time goes on, what has been found is that if you aren't open, conscious, and aware—in other words if your bubble turns from light, free-flowing, and translucent into a force field—it can remain that way for a long time. If you remain in your bubble but never really truly see or learn about anything else or anyone else in the world, you will turn your bubble into a wall.

I often think, why do people want to stay in the confinement of a bubble? Why would they want to remain enclosed in that force field? These folks are happy to remain in their bubbles and do not want to learn about the beautiful, diverse world around them. They are stuck.

Then there are others who are curious, wondering, and just don't know where to begin to stretch outside of their bubbles to learn or unlearn what has been taught to them.

Lastly, there is a group of people whose bubbles are always porous, meshing with other bubbles. They have learned or are still learning about themselves and others. They have always lived a life of being open, curious, and wondering.

When someone wants to stay inside of their bubble, it is because the bubble is comfortable, reliable, and sustainable. Yes, all of those things keep folks in their own bubbles, and it can feel good—until it doesn't. It can feel good until you realize that over time your heart has hardened and is no longer open.

Educators, parents, and students, it's time to pop out of our bubbles because our world with all its diverse people is a beautiful space just waiting for the popping to begin—to learn, to grow, to change, to expand.

Reading and Your Bubble

Reading is one of the best ways to step outside of your bubble. Taking the time to read and learn about true history, other cultures, races, origins, communities, and especially marginalized communities is a way to step outside your bubble. This doesn't mean you are losing who you are or that you are threatening your own bubble, but it does mean that reading and learning outside your bubble might make you move in this world differently. It might mean you show up differently when thinking about communities and races outside of your bubble. It could even mean that you take a stand against the injustices that marginalized communities face. You might be thinking, wait, all because of a book or books that I have read? Well, yes. That is where we can begin.

Reading is power, and reading outside your bubble is even more powerful. One of the many teachings of the great Frederick Douglass was that literacy is the path from slavery to freedom. Douglass said, "Once you learn to read, you will forever be free." At the time, Douglass was speaking of enslaved Black folks where the right to read was stripped from them. But in today's world, when reading is a right to us all, isn't staying in your bubble keeping you from freedom? Isn't not knowing the truth about our world—the injustices yesterday and today—a form of slavery because it forces you to stay in your bubble? Reading is a power that we often take for granted. We take for granted this right we have, our freedom, because it is easy to stay within our bubbles—it's easy to stay comfortable and ignore what is going on around us. It is easy to ignore it especially if you aren't part of the marginalized communities. But it is time. It is past time to read outside of our bubbles, to make changes. It is time because our world, our communities, our children are relying on us to help create a world where reading outside of our bubbles is the norm and not just a form of deviance or radicalism. Reading outside our bubbles is a way to connect us all.

Making a Change

As an educator, I have always had the desire to learn about other cultures, races, and folks who were different from me, but my bubble was really stretched when I was pushed to think deeply about particular books by an author who I had to remove from my day-to-day use as an elementary school teacher and as a mother.

Those books were written by Theodor Seuss Geisel—you may know him as Dr. Seuss. I grew up with Dr. Seuss. I taught with Dr. Seuss. I even dressed up as Dr. Seuss during Read Across America in 2010. How could I possibly change my mind about an author who had a place in my childhood reading journey and had even spilled over into my teaching year after year? Some of you may be thinking, good for you (especially if you have read and know his problematic history). Or some of you may be even thinking, how you could possibly let go of rhyming, colorful, creative, innovative Dr. Seuss?

I began releasing Dr. Seuss when I was privy to his racist past as a cartoonist and the hidden and sometimes blatant racism in some of his books. I read a study entitled "The Cat Is Out of the Bag: Orientalism, Anti-Blackness, and White Supremacy in Dr. Seuss' Children's Books" by Katie Ishizuka and

Ramón Stephens. I remember this stretching of my bubble like it was yesterday. I was sent Ishizuka and Stephans' study by a friend after I posted on social media about a Seuss book that I was highlighting and a picture of me dressed as Cat in the Hat. They privately shared the link to this study with me. They called me in with love. As I began reading this study, my heart sank. I felt my gut clench. I was disappointed and angry by what I was reading about a long-time favorite author that I loved.

After I had finished reading this study. I didn't just leave it there. I didn't just read the study alone but decided to do my own research after reading this disheartening piece. To my surprise, there it was—the truth. I saw through my own research the pictures of Dr. Seuss in blackface, the racist drawings of people of Asian culture, and the embedded white supremacy in his books—books that I had once loved. It was all there.

I began to take time to question why I loved Dr. Seuss so much. I began to do some soul-searching about the roots that were dug so deep, and I began to look at other options to replace the books of his that I always loved. I had to slow down and really ask myself what it was about Dr. Seuss' books that drew me in? It was the colorfulness of the pages, the "funny" characters, the silly rhyming, and the playfulness. I realized that there were so many books that I loved that had those things embedded and more. As I began stripping my shelves both at home and at school of these books, I realized I no longer wanted to remain blinded or stuck. I realized I wanted to know more about history, about other cultures, and about other things I had not been privy to or that had been hidden.

I began to search for books that showed other characters, other cultures, other communities, and other stories. I wanted to know more and teach my learnings to my own kids and my students. And guess what? I found them. There were so many authors—diverse authors—who included all of the things I loved about reading Dr. Seuss' books while allowing their readers to feel seen and other stories to be told. And their books were honestly better. The work I did to release my childhood attachment to Dr. Seuss was not hard work, but it was intentional work. It was internal work that went through a process of acceptance—a process of shedding.

My first step in the process was listening, next was learning, and then came full-on acceptance, taking time to dig into my emotions around the truth that was uncovered, making the decision to find more truth, there was a release and a pop of the bubble through listening, reading, and learning. The last step of my learning was taking action. It was work that took time and work that was ongoing. The stretching and popping of my own bubble had to begin with myself first;

everyone has their own journey. However, we are at a time in our society where popping and reading outside of your own bubble is critical. It is critical to our world and to the safety and lives of others.

The metaphor of a person stepping outside their bubble means to take a person out of their comfort zone—what they are used to—and it brings them to a new way of thinking, a new way of beginning to move in the world, a transformation process, and, for educators, a change in the way they teach. Although I know that it seems like a simple metaphor, it is one that I used to get outside of myself and into the worlds of others. It's a place where I find the most stretching, the most thoughtfulness, and the most discomfort. That discomfort is where growth can live. That discomfort is where the transformation can occur to break out of the force fields that we have allowed to remain for so long. It is that "stuckness."

When I stopped using Dr. Seuss' books in my classroom, it still took me some time to share with others the reason why. I was afraid of what others would say or do to me if I voiced other options rather than a "Seuss-themed" Read Across America week or that I didn't want to celebrate his birthday or read and share the books of a man who was a racist. It was fear that was embedded in being one of the only people standing up for what needed to change. I realized that standing up for truth was bigger than my fear. I had to do it even if I had to do it alone, and I had to do it even if my voice quivered.

I got into this education game to make a difference, but how could I make a difference if I was afraid? So, I spoke up and I spoke out. I provided other diverse alternatives to Read Across America week. I shared the changes that the National Education Association had begun making to truly Read Across America through diverse books without Seuss being at the center. It felt good to speak up. I knew it was the right thing to do even if I was doing it alone. I knew it was the right thing to do even when my voice trembled. I knew it was what was in the best interest for all children for them to read outside their bubbles, to know the truth, and to learn how to move in this world differently.

Why Should We Read Beyond Our Bubbles?

Thinking about my story and the purpose behind it makes me think about the times before my Dr. Seuss release, when I didn't think twice about the pushback or the repercussions of me reading a book outside the bubbles of my students. I have always wanted to ensure that my students and my own children had the opportunities to learn about themselves (in their bubbles) but also learn about someone or something different from how they identified in this world. I have always wanted to encourage my students and my own children to be okay and comfortable with reading, listening, and learning outside their bubbles. This was my goal of not only teaching students to learn to read, but also to build readers who want to be better people who want to learn about other folks different from them and build relationships and connections with others outside of their bubbles.

There was never any pushback in providing opportunities for my students to learn to read and to be a lifelong reader. I believe most educators have that vision and mission in the work that we do. We know that this work is purposeful work. It is also just as important to be very intentional about ensuring that our students are reading beyond themselves. Today, this is vital work for everyone to take on—especially for the new generations to come. Reading beyond what you normally read is reading outside your bubble. The urgency of this is so critical to our communities, our spaces, and our world. Getting to know other people and cultures that are different from who we are and how we move in this world is critical to cultivating empathy and compassion for others. It makes our world a better place to live in.

However, in the most recent years after the 2020 reckoning, there has been an extreme increase in pushback when reading books that are diverse, inclusive, about Black folks, about people of color, and those who identify as LGTBQ+. There has been a fear that has been planted by society and the powers that be through book bans and creation of "policies" for educators to read books to children that are outside their bubbles. It is sad and troublesome, but it is the truth of the world. We live in a society where the past is covered up to make people feel better. But covering up the truth of the past is not the goal—at least it isn't for me.

Learning about history, the stories of others, and others who may be different from my bubble is the important work that we need to get into, and we can use diverse and inclusive literature to begin that digging. This is where we can begin to make changes and transformations through the pages of a book. But even deeper than reading the pages in a book is engulfing yourself in the stories of the people within those books. That is what can get at the heart of a person. It is reading outside our bubbles that makes this possible. It is the reading of the stories and listening to the stories of others that creates impact.

Beginning to Step Outside Your Bubble

To begin to stretch outside your bubble, you need to start learning about differences and cultures outside of it. Slow down, read and listen to others, and be open to differences.

You have to get to know yourself deeply and be committed to getting to know others with that same energy and curiosity. That means having an open heart and open mind and looking at yourself and areas to improve. In Chapter 4 of this book, I talk about using the LEAP framework to begin integrating inclusive text in your everyday lessons for students. It is a framework to begin reading, learning, and teaching outside your bubble. As you continue this journey, the following are some common ideas to keep in mind and reflect on as you are reading and learning.

Release Bias and Judgment of Differences

Bias is prejudice in favor of or against one thing, person, or group compared with another. I look at bias as a judgment of differences and stereotypes. I am *this* and you are not—you are *that*. To be that is not what/who I am, so it is not okay to be that. I also look at it as I am this, and this is much better than that. Does that make sense? It's your bubble.

Your bubble can hold those biases. This means that we all have biases that we have to release. We all have areas to work on to dispel these biases. But it does in fact take ongoing work and ongoing learning. The first step of stretching outside the bubble is to acknowledge your biases and recognize that we all have them. Being honest with ourselves is essential. Take time to reflect on your biases and how they might be affecting your thoughts, feelings, and behaviors toward others.

Next, take time to learn more about different cultures, identities, and perspectives. I will discuss more about that in the following chapters. Take time to slow down and practice empathy and question your assumptions. Those are some basic steps to take as you begin to release biases. The reason I say begin is because this is a constant journey and not a destination. Once we believe we are healed and we are fully released from a bias, another bias surfaces that we didn't know was even present. So we begin the releasing process again and continue the journey of learning and growing because, guess what, we are always learning and growing.

Be Open to Learning and Growing

This is something that has been instilled in me since I was a child by my mother, my father, and my family. I was taught that I have never "arrived" and that there is always room to learn, grow, and even change. As an educator, through my years of schooling in this field, being a learner is not something new to most of us. However, I am aware that not everyone believes this. Not everyone is as open to learning and growing as others. Some of us may say we are, but that is not the action taken. Some hold tightly to our bubbles when we feel that it may change us in the way we operate, the way we move, the way we think—change who we are at our core.

But that openness to learning and growing is where changes in the most positive way can happen. It is where we can take some time to look outside ourselves to be better for us and the next generation. It is where we can reach outside of our bubbles, pick up a book (one we wouldn't normally pick up), and read it. It is where we can learn and grow. It is where we can take that learning and extend it to others. It is what is needed to become more open to learning. It allows that curiosity to lead and that wonder to guide—guide you to the openness to read, learn, and see a world beyond your bubble. As educators, it is pertinent that we remain teachable and open to learning. We have a great responsibility to our students and fellow colleagues in the work we do.

I do not know about you, but I got into education to change the world, one drop at a time. I am unsure how close I am to this transformation, but one thing I do know for certain is that I have placed many drops along my teaching journey in this world. That must count for something. Another thing I know for sure is that I continue to remain a learner and stretch myself outside of my bubble often. That must count for something too. Many drops along the way. That is my goal.

Be Okay with Feeling Uncomfortable

You may feel uneasy or uncomfortable when you begin to stretch yourself outside of your bubble. That is normal. For me, I have encountered hard conversations, especially centered around my race, my identity, my color, my family, and my culture, more often than I care to count. I specifically remember the feeling that initially arose when those microaggressions, which sadly I was used to encountering—mostly at work, turned into macroaggressions. I distinctly remember when my Black son was racially profiled at a local park by cops at the age of 14. I shared about the encounter. I shared my hurt, my fear, and my anger, and instead of being listened to, I was verbally attacked. Even in the midst of anger and disappointment, I still spoke up—for my son and myself.

There were many other times when I felt uncomfortable, which was rooted in fear, sadness, anger, and disappointment. I would feel it in my body, my gut, my sweaty pits, my clammy hands, and my stomach, and yet, I felt I didn't have a choice but to speak up for myself and for other marginalized folks around me. That feeling of not having a choice, as a Black woman, is definitely something that most Black folks and people of color face.

But if you are not BIPOC, then in this case, having the choice to pop out of your bubble is a privilege. However, I have seen and been privy to how the use of that privilege and power can be used in positive ways and used by those who have read, learned, and grown outside of their bubbles. And we have come to a time and place where it is critical to read and learn outside of our bubbles.

Get yourself in a place where you are okay with being uncomfortable—take it in and accept it. And even if you aren't okay with the feelings, push through them and do it even if you are afraid. Read outside your bubble even if you have a fear of learning. Read outside your bubble even if it is hard to learn about true history due to the emotions that may arise. Read outside your bubble to learn about and celebrate races, cultures, and communities different from your own. You will still be the core of who you are and a better version of that core, one who wants to listen in, read, learn, and take action outside of your bubble.

Build a Community and a Connection with Others

Reading outside of your bubble is only an initial step to learning and growing as an individual, a person, and a human. It is important to take time to reach, listen, and learn about others outside of your bubble by building a community and connection with others who may be different from you. There are so many times when I am looking at social media and the pictures that people post, and it is glaring how many people don't have a diverse group of friends.

I can see from the pictures posted where the diversity is lacking. I see pictures where folks are in their own bubbles—their bubbles of comfortability. I have even taken the time to scroll through their friend lists (tons of folks are now going to block me from their lists—enter chuckle). I have seen a lack of diversity there as well, and at first I was shocked. I was disappointed, and now I realize—folks are in their bubbles. Have you taken the time to scroll and reflect on the friends on your lists? Have you taken the time to see just how diverse your community is? Have you taken the time to reach out to folks who may be in your communities, at work, at school, at church, or at social events, and truly taken time to build community and connection with them?

I am not saying that this is the time to begin adding folks to your friends list or overstepping boundaries. But I do urge you to allow it to happen in a natural, authentic way. It is one way to take time to learn from other folks who are outside of your bubble. It is one way to stretch outside your reading, your learning, and tap into community with others. This will be a step in the right direction to listen to their stories, believe the stories, and learn from them.

The great Audre Lorde says, "Without community, there is no liberation . . . but community must not mean a shedding of our differences, nor the pathetic pretense that these differences do not exist" (Lorde, 1984). We want to connect with others and build community with others to listen, learn, and celebrate. It is that interconnectedness that will make us stronger and more intentional learners.

In the midst of your learning, you will make mistakes. I am not saying it might happen—it will happen. You will say something that is messed up, and you will have to take accountability for it, apologize authentically, continue learning, and make a shift. We have all been there or will be there at some point. We are all human. We all mess up. This shouldn't stop you from reading, learning, growing, and building the community needed in order to build a better world and better place for us all. Mistakes are another opportunity to learn, grow, and be better— better for ourselves, for others, for students, and for our children.

The Time Is Now

With more and more books being banned every day, it is time to take action. Actually it is past the time. We have control over what we read, what we learn, how we build community, and the connections we make with others. That is the first step. It is the first step into reading outside your bubbles. It is the first step into making the world a better place for all of us—but especially our children and our students.

I know that society has its way of placing a sense of fear inside of you to read outside your bubble or teach students outside of theirs, but reading is where your power lies and learning about others different from ourselves; that is where the power lies. Without it we become powerless. It is important that we realize and are attuned to what is happening around us, in our schools, in our school districts, and in our communities.

Taking away the books and silencing the voices, the stories, and the history of those from marginalized communities takes away the inclusivity and beauty of our world. It takes away the sense of belonging to our world. It takes away the acknowledgment and the celebration of our differences. It is essential that we take this time to truly pay attention, to evaluate what is happening in society, and to keep our eyes open, our ears pierced, and our hearts and our minds alert. We must be aware of what is happening. Sometimes when policies are created, the policymakers expect folks to not know about policy or voting that take place at school board meetings. Get the information you need to stay aware because the time is now.

Taking Action to Step Outside Your Bubble

In the upcoming chapters, we are going to move through actionable steps to truly begin this process of reading outside our bubbles. Because yes, there is a process. We will move through what it looks like to really dig into what Dr. Rudine Sims Bishop said, "books are sometimes windows, offering views of worlds that may be real or imagined, familiar, or strange. These windows are also sliding glass doors, and readers have only to walk through to become part of whatever world has been

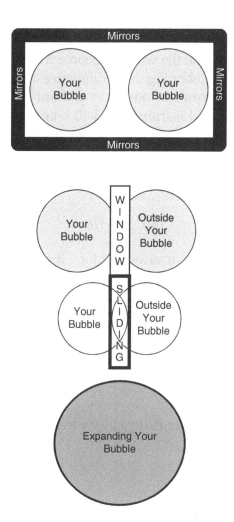

Figure 1.1 Providing mirrors, windows, and sliding-glass doors for yourself and others

created or re-created by the author. When lighting conditions are just right, how-ever, a window can also be a mirror. Literature transforms human experience and reflects it back to us, and in that reflection, we can see our own lives and expe-riences as part of a larger human experience. Reading, then, becomes a means of self-affirmation, and readers often seek their mirrors in books" (https://www .readingrockets.org/sites/default/files/migrated/Mirrors-Windows-and-Sliding-Glass-Doors.pdf).

Figure 1.1 gives insight of what it can look like to provide mirrors, windows, and sliding-glass doors for yourself and others. As you read the upcoming chap-ters, you will learn what it takes to open those windows for us and our students to read outside of our translucent bubbles. We will learn actionable steps to see what it looks like to slide into the world of people who may be different than we are, while learning and celebrating those differences. From there, we will learn what it takes to create mirrors for ourselves and our students—our children in our day-to-day teaching and learning. We will take time to learn how to culti-vate community—because we are better and stronger together, in community. Community is where lasting change lies. Let's dig in and take this learning journey together.

Let's Reflect

1. What is something you have advocated for, even when fearful?

2. After reading this chapter, what type of inside-your-bubble work have you done?

3. Do you feel that you need to read and learn more about yourself and your identity inside your own bubble? What steps do you need to take to do that?

4. What are your beliefs when you think about reading outside your bub-ble? What are your beliefs when you think about students reading outside their bubbles?

5. Take time to recall a mistake that you have made. What did you do to recover from that mistake?

Chapter 2
Expand Your Relationship Bubble: Relationships and Reading

Relationships

Reading outside your bubble is just the beginning, and it's an ongoing work. But as a teacher or leader in schools, we know that reading outside our bubbles is not the ultimate goal. Don't get me wrong, reading within and outside our bubbles is essential. It is essential in learning how to read and write about books critically, to connect with them, to take in and learn about ourselves, and to learn about the lives and perspectives of others. However, we cannot move into deeper actions, such as actions to change beliefs or cultivate care, compassion, concern, and empathy, without relationships. There is a human side to reading outside our bubbles, where we connect with others and, especially as an educator, where we connect with students. We must build the relationships with students in our learning communities in order for reading outside our bubbles to make a difference in the lives of our students and in the lives of ourselves. If you read outside your bubble just to learn about yourself and others and ***still*** remain physically and emotionally inside your own bubble, how can true transformation be made? How can we use inclusive, diverse books, as the power sources that they are to change the world? That might be a lofty goal, but it is a goal that I have with ultimate hope and faith that it can and will happen—eventually. We need a shift in our world and a shift into who we can be. The shift has to come from within, and the shift has to be made in relationships we cultivate day to day.

It takes expanding our bubbles in our homes, in our schools/learning communities, outside our homes, and in the communities in which we live. It begins with building relationships. Relationships hold the power to take our steps from reading outside our bubbles into the expansion of other folks' bubbles into our lives. It takes it from being something that we just are "supposed to do" into something that we are doing for ourselves and others. It takes opening up our world through books. It can begin in our homes in the families we build and grow. It can begin in our classrooms in the faces that we see each and every day. We can expand our bubbles by getting to know the beautiful faces that step through the doors of our learning communities. It has to begin somewhere. That somewhere starts with us. It starts with our community.

Community Is the Heart

Community is the heart of everything we do. It is in the community where we can learn about one another, connect, celebrate, and understand one another. Thích Nhất Hanh, a Vietnamese Thiền Buddhist monk, peace activist, prolific author, poet, and teacher, has said, "Community is the core of everything. Community is where there should be harmony and peace and understanding. That is something created by our daily life together. If love exists in the community, if we've been nourished by the harmony in the community, then we will never move away from love," (Bell Hooks, 2017). By having a community in which there is authentic harmony, peace, and understanding threaded within it, relationships will be built. These relationships will be built on love. The word *love* has become a word that we reserve only for our closest humans. But what if we looked at our community as communities that allow love, peace, and harmony to permeate through them? We must allow that thread of love to move through our own bubbles first. Then we expand that love to the bubbles of others. It doesn't just have to show up with the folks most close to us—it can be cultivated and grown in the community in which we learn. It can be cultivated in our immersion in the inclusive books we read. Inclusive books offer truth in our history and stories of the unheard.

Ways to Build Community in the Classroom

Community building in the classroom is a way to expand your relationship bubble—the action alongside reading outside your bubble. We need to expand our bubbles with other folks if we really want reading outside our bubbles to matter in the way we move throughout the world. There are a variety of ways that you can build community in the classroom. One of the ways you can build community is to create an environment in which all students feel safe. That means creating a sense of belonging, acceptance, openness, and care with all of our students. It means allowing students to have a voice in your classroom. It can also mean allowing the students to collaborate to make classroom agreements, norms, and decisions. Building classroom communities also helps to cultivate relationships and expand your bubble as the educator but also for your students.

When I previously taught fifth grade, I remember my students coming into my classroom with a wall up and not wanting to let others in to get to know them. They struggled to open up, and when they did, they were defensive and didn't want to share. I'm sure it was because they did not trust me—yet. I needed to connect with them for this to happen. The more we met in our community circles and the more that students could see that I valued their voices in our learning community, they began to open up, and their walls began to tumble down. They began to trust me. They began to trust that I meant what I said and I showed what I meant. They knew I cared about them.

Children are great observers. My students watched as I asked the class whether we should make our literacy block a little longer due to some students not understanding the concept. They agreed to make it longer—together. And we did. Students would watch when I would ask the class's opinion on what we should do as a class celebration—and we decided together. They realized in these small, but mighty, moments, that their voices were valued, because I listened and heard them. When they began to believe that, they began to use their voices more in our classroom community. They began to feel safe and open to be who they are.

Let's Cultivate Love in Our Community—In Our Relationships

Taking the first step to cultivate love in our learning/school community is a step toward building relationships. But what could that look/sound/feel like? Black author, theorist, educator, and social critic Bell Hooks tells us in *All About Love* (Hooks, 2000) that "love is an action, a participatory emotion. Whether we are engaged in a process of self-love or of loving others we must move beyond the realm of feeling to actualize love." That can happen in our learning communities. Actualizing love in a school community can look and feel like taking time to get to know the students in your learning community beyond just the surface level—this shows care and affection. It can sound like being an advocate for students to feel seen in the learning community and in the books that they pick up from the shelves—this shows care and commitment. It can look and sound like teaching from inclusive texts in lessons and learning that incorporates mirrors, windows, and sliding glass doors—this shows recognition, care, and commitment to the people and communities that the students are learning about. It can look like teaching true history from multiple perspectives—this shows honest and open communication. Hooks states that to truly love we must learn to mix care, affection, recognition, respect, commitment, and trust, as well as honest and open communication. These are examples that help to love, build trust, and expand your relationship bubble in your learning community while you are also expanding your bubble through reading, connecting, learning, and growing. These elements are core ingredients as we build and maintain relationships with our students.

Community Meetings + Reading + Connecting Outside Your Bubbles

One thing I have always done, when leading the classroom, was to have community meetings. They began as morning meetings in all levels of my teaching. I transitioned to calling them community meetings because the meetings would occur at other times of the day and not just in the morning. I remember the first time I called my fifth graders, the "seniors" of the school, to my carpet for a community meeting. They looked at me like I had three heads. Them? Fifth graders going to the carpet to sit? I motioned for them to come to the carpet and sit in a circle. Sitting in a circle, myself included, has a powerful meaning. It fosters connection. Sitting in a circle creates a sense of belonging and inclusivity. It allows everyone to have the same level of power in the group while being a part of the circle. The circle is also a symbol of unity—without a beginning or ending, it continues on. The circle can begin to create psychological safety where feelings of trust, tenderness, compassion, and braveness can be ignited. So, yes, my fifth-graders listened, they came into the circle, and they sat. My fifth graders and I sat in a circle. I introduced our community meetings as a place for us to build community together. We would talk, share, and connect. Sometimes I would begin with a quote, and we would discuss what is meant to each of us. Other times, I would read a portion of a book, and we would discuss it and connect. I would also ask a question for each of us to answer, and sometimes students would lead the meetings. I wanted them to feel that our meetings were not just about me but about our community as a whole. I also shared that this meeting was a way to provide a space to just be ourselves, to learn about others, and to grow together as a community.

Once I explained what the meetings were, we took time to create agreements for the meetings. We created agreements to ensure that we had equity of voice, respected one another, listened, kept an open mind and heart, and didn't speak over one another. We created these agreements collaboratively, and it was powerful. We continued to have these meetings each day. They lasted for 10–15 minutes. Community meetings helped students to build relationships with each other, as well as for me to build relationships with my students, and for them to learn, read, and discuss outside their bubbles.

Getting to Know the Students in Your Learning Community

Take the time to get to know your students within your learning community. Allowing them to get to know you while you simultaneously get to know them is invaluable to students feeling safe, seen, and valuable in the learning community. Gholdy Muhammad in her book *Unearthing Joy* states, "We cannot teach who we don't know (Muhammad, 2023). Nor can we teach students to know themselves, their consciousness, or their joy if we don't know ourselves, our consciousness, or our joy" (2023)

Getting to know who your students are is a critical part of teaching, and doing this even before you get to know your students as readers/learners is essential. This allows your students to know that you see them at their core and not just on an academic level. Doing this authentically is going to be a game changer for not just in their reading but for the entire year or years of learning with your students. Learning who they are is so critical—for them and for you. When a student knows that you see them and understand what is important to them, they will move mountains in their learning journeys. Yes, we want students to read outside their bubbles, and we want them to learn outside them, too. But we have to get to know our students well for them to feel the work—the action behind reading outside your bubble and reading outside their bubbles. There is more at the root of learning; it's about relationships. As Gloria Ladson-Billings states:

> [Teachers need to] know enough about students' cultural and individual lifecircumstances to be able to communicate well with them. They understand the need to study the students because they believe there is something there worth

learning. They know that students who have the academic and cultural where-with-al to succeed in school without losing their identities are better prepared to be of service to others; in a democracy, this commitment to the public good is paramount. (Ladson-Billings, 2001)

This commitment is what it is about. Yes, we want them to learn and do so with rigor and passion, and we also want our students to be of service to others in the world we live in. This is the work that teachers who want to make a difference do—this is our work.

Let's Visualize

Think about a teacher who you really connected with in school. Close your eyes and visualize their face, how they moved, what they said. You can see that teacher so clearly, right? Now, I want you to think about a time of connection or maybe even what made you remember that teacher. That teacher for me was Mrs. Poledor, my fifth-grade teacher. Mrs. Poledor was my first Black teacher since preschool. To be honest, I don't remember much of anything she taught me that year other than declarative and interrogative sentences. She sang and danced those words to a tune—that I will remember forever. Even though I was a reader who struggled with fluency and comprehension, I remember my fifth-grade year was when I fell madly in love with reading. I also remember sitting in her class-room during a parent–teacher conference between her and my mother. During that conference, I remember her telling my mother not to worry about her baby and that she would take care of me. Care. She would care for me. I will tell you one thing. She did not lie to my mother during that conference.

I absolutely felt the care of Mrs. Poledor throughout the entire year. When I struggled in math, she cared and helped me get extra help. When I would strug-gle in reading, she would work with me and help me to understand. All of these attributes of Mrs. Poledor showed me that she was teaching with love, concern, compassion, and care. I knew she loved me, and I knew she loved teaching. With-out the relationship, I don't think that I would have pushed myself as much as I did in fifth grade. Prior to being in her classroom, I was one of the students that would do just enough to get by—I wasn't pushed in school by my teachers prior to Mrs. Poledor. I was good with just enough—and so were my teachers. My mother also pushed me, and with both by my side, that year I did better than just enough.

Without the relationship that Mrs. Poledor built with me, I don't know if I would have trusted her enough to let her know that I didn't understand or comprehend what I was reading, but I did. I trusted Mrs. Poledor. I trusted that when she handed me a book that I could see myself in, see that mirror, that I read it and love it. I trusted her. That made all the difference. Did Mrs. Poledor sit and ask me a ton of interview-type questions to connect with me? No. Our relationship happened in many connections—not just in one sitting. Our relationship happened in what she said and what she showed all of her students through her actions. It happened when she gave me her time—even if it was a short amount of time, and she was always present and always loving. It wasn't just me that she did this with; she did this with all the students in her classes. We felt loved by her, and because of that love and care, I enjoyed coming to school, and I loved learning from her. I believe my other classmates did, too.

When you think about the students in your learning community, how can you cultivate that type of relationship with them? That Poledor relationship. It does not have to look exactly like what I shared because we are all different. All relationships will be different and have a different dynamic. What is the same is that there is nothing like teaching from the foundation of love, care, authenticity, and giving students the gift of time. Giving time to your students, even if it is for a moment, means so much to your students and inherently it will mean so much to you as well. As you take the time with students and get to know them, do so without judgment. Allow them to show up as who they are—with all the intersections of the identities they hold. Allow them to bring who they are to the learning environment, and you bring your authentic self too. "Being yourself and allowing your students to also bring their full selves into the learning community is important to building a strong teacher-to-student relationship" (Creekmore & Creekmore, 2024). Building the relationship with your students helps to open the connection between knowing your students and who they are. Knowing who they are allows you to truly see them first and foremost—even before teaching them. When you see them, then it is easier to include them as you continue to build your learning community together. A learning community includes the students and who they are in the environment, the lessons, the materials, the books that you use, and the books that they read. You have the students you serve in mind and those you may not serve yet in mind as you begin your planning journey. When I say students you may not serve, I mean that even students who may not be sitting in the chairs of your classrooms also need to be valued, uplifted, and their stories still need to be heard, learned, shared, and discussed—especially if you have a class of predominantly white students. What you are providing for those students are windows. You are sliding the glass doors open for them to see into the worlds of others. Those stories and perspectives may even be mirrors—because some mirrors could be unknown by you as the teacher, and yet, they are there. You are providing a mirror to a student that needs it—often even when you don't know it.

I worked in a school of predominantly white students, as one of the only three Black teachers in the school. I felt it was pertinent that I provided the students with books, learnings, and text that expanded their bubbles. I wanted to expand their bubbles outside of the standards that were taught. The standards are often one-sided and share only one narrative. I knew that including in their learning a variety of perspectives would allow for the students to see past their individual bubbles and look outside of themselves into the lives of others—specifically others who live in the margins of what society sees as the "norm." The students wanted to learn outside their bubbles. They were engaged and excited to read outside their bubbles. This is your duty as an educator to help to transform who we are collectively. Part of that transformation is opening the world to your students. You can do that by reading outside your bubble, by having your students read outside there's, and by taking that learning into action. That is what I did with my students. I showed them I cared by getting to know each of them and expanding their bubbles. I wanted to introduce them to worlds outside of their own.

Knowing Your Students as Readers

Reading outside your bubble is initiated by beginning with self first. I will talk more about this important component later. However, you must know your students well, and that includes knowing them as readers. It includes knowing their reading experience and background. What does literacy look like in their homes, in their families, in their communities, or in their cultures? For instance, in some cultures, storytelling is valued and respected. Knowing your students as readers and storytellers is an important component that should be embedded in your teaching—in their learning in school and throughout life. Knowing your students as readers also means knowing where they are developmentally in their reading—even if they are beginning readers. This means knowing how motivated and engaged they are when reading, either for themselves or when others are reading aloud to them. We want our students to actually enjoy reading and be excited to read and motivated to do so. Knowing students as readers includes language comprehension, which includes background knowledge (cultural competence, content knowledge, reading specific, etc.). The background knowledge we need as teachers and the background they need as they learn and grow as readers of text can help to cultivate and expand their cultural and content knowledge in the process of taking text and expanding their bubbles.

Comprehension is also an important component to know your students as readers. We want our students to be able to read and understand the text they read at high levels. Reading and comprehending outside your bubble can help build the background knowledge to connect to a variety of texts, but it also allows for your students to connect with others. As an educator, it is important to know how your students recognize words and bridge the processes in reading including print concepts, reading fluency, vocabulary knowledge, etc. (Duke & Cartwright, 2021). Knowing your students as readers involves a number of components; however, knowing who they are as readers allows you as the teacher to know them well and teach them well. That knowledge of how your students read, as well as their areas of strength and their areas of growth, will be important to teachers of reading as well as teachers who teach all content areas.

My son was not the kid who had the most books in his room. As an avid reader, owner, and lover of books, I didn't understand why. He was a lover of math and science but not a fan of reading at all. I wanted him to read more. He was going into the ninth grade, and it was summer, and I wanted him to read a book over the summer. I knew (because he is my son lol) he is a lover of basketball. So you know what I did, I looked for books I could find about basketball. Through my search I found Kwame Alexander, the author of the book *The Crossover*. I bought the book for me and him to buddy read together and discuss. He absolutely loved that book and so did I. He read it in three days, faster than I could finish. We had in-depth discussions about the book, and when the prequel came out, *Rebound*, my son read that book, too! He also introduced the books to his younger sister, who also read it. This should show you how important it is to know your readers, what their interests are, and how your excitement and engagement in books can also increase other students', or my son's or daughter's in this instance, excitement and engagement as well.

Reading Chats

Even though it was summer, my son and I had reading discussions about the books or comic books he read. You can also have reading discussions or individual lessons in your classroom. I have always believed that having this type of teacher-to-student learning creates connection. These are also what I like to call reading chats. I call them chats because I don't want it to seem as though it's a question/answer session or to have test-like feeling. I want it to be a conversation—but a time where learning can also take place. I often would do these reading chats while they are reading independently, but it could happen in a small group as well. I ask them about the book they are reading, why the book was chosen, what their take was on the book, what they learned, their thinking, etc. These questions as we chat can also involve asking about the evolving characters in the text, the character's background, the choices the characters make in the text. During the chat, I am truly discussing and evaluating what the student is taking in as they read. I want to know how they are conceptualizing the text and their opinions about what they are reading. This allows me to truly get to know my students, their thought process as they read, and their level of comprehension. I also will ask the student to continue reading with me. Reading chats provide information on engagement, motivation, comprehension, reading skills, and overall understanding of the text they are reading. Students must understand the text they are reading to be able to connect with the text, expand their bubbles, and do some perspective-taking. Those are some components that help us get to know our students as readers. They also help me to build relationships with my students. It helps me to see them as humans, as learners, and as readers. It provides me with the information needed to facilitate learning with them in real time. Especially since the student should be reading outside their bubbles, it allows me to hear their learning through perspective-taking while reading and discussing the text. Reading chats offer the gift of reading outside your bubble and moving into actionable steps to getting to know your students, which is part of the process of expanding your bubble. This happens through the relationship-building that takes place in the classroom community as well as one-on-one with your students.

Reading Partners

Reading partners is another great way to get to know your students as readers. Partners in reading help us to get to know how our students interact with other readers, the other students in the learning community. It also helps us learn more about our students as learners. Taking time to discuss and model with students what reading partners should look and sound like is going to be essential as you teach your readers how to move through reading partners effectively. During reading partners, most of the time the students are partnering on the same text. Whether they are taking time to buddy-read or have read the text prior to partnering, having them read the same text is beneficial to being able to have a rich conversation. The partners can be grouped in different ways. Students can choose their own reading partners. This way is helpful to see socially how the students in your class naturally connect with each other in smaller social groups. You can find out a lot from who chooses one another. I have used this way to learn who my students gravitate to and who gets left out of the choosing. My purpose here is learning about group dynamics during reading time. Another way I have also implemented reading partners in my classroom is where I place students together who have some of the same goals and growth areas in reading. This provides some information about the students who are growing and learning together. Sometimes I find that this works, and other times, I have found that both students have a difficult time moving through the text, comprehending the text, and discussing the text with one another. During these moments, I have pulled the students together with me in a small group to move through the text with my scaffolding alongside them. I have also created reading partners who have different growth areas and different strengths. This is one way students can be teachers and learners collaboratively. I love to see students teaching and learning from each other. This not only allows me to get to know them but also allows them to get to know each other as reading partners in class. It allows them to build relationships in our learning community. In doing that, we are strengthening our learning community.

Expand Your Everyday

Expanding your bubble by taking the time to get to know your students is important. Taking time to get to know who you are and the people around you is essential too. Expanding outside of your bubble means just that—the growth. This might be a push for some a little bit. As I said earlier, this is not just reading outside your bubble as a surface-level action but a truly deeper shift in how we move in society. It is a shift in how we show up not just at work as educators, not just for our students but in how we show up in life. It is a push for us to expand our bubbles in our lifestyles.

That could look like getting to know folks that don't look like you. It means, for example, moving from "I don't see color" to actually seeing color—and celebrating it. It is seeing the person in front of you as a human being that deserves celebration. That celebration comes from reading, learning, and connecting with others. The spirit of expanding outside of your bubble is at its root—the compassion, the connection, and the community. It could possibly look like connecting with others who may not believe what you believe. You can learn from others who do not believe what you believe, and you can even find commonalities within your varying belief systems. Yes, that can happen. Take time to think about what expanding outside your bubbles could look like daily for you. What could you do to expand in other areas of your life? It could look like having coffee or tea with a neighbor who may have been living next door to you for two years, and all you do is smile and wave. It could look like having your children play with children and befriend children who have identity markers different from them. This may take intentionality on your part, and sometimes (if you are part introvert like me) it may push you, and the push, although it may feel uncomfortable, is not a bad thing. Get comfortable with feeling uncomfortable. It is okay, and it is for the greater good. It is a human-centered approach to living. If this is how you move on a day-to-day basis, then this will ultimately feed into your classroom with students. Expanding your bubbles outside of the classroom will help you as the educator to be more intentional about that expansion inside your classrooms. It will allow you to tap into curiosity, as well as authentic knowing, learning, and compassion. What once took intentionality to engage in will now be innate. But it has to begin somewhere, and it has to be somewhere that you want to be. Our students deserve to be known as readers, learners, and humans. Expanding outside of your bubbles through living each and every day will make reading outside of your bubbles that much more impactful—it will make teaching to include books outside of the "normative" bubbles that much more impactful. It can begin to change the world—one step at a time through the relationships we build and our openness to being a learner.

Let's Reflect

1. What are ways that you build relationships with your students in your learning community?
2. Do you believe it is important to expand your bubble outside your classroom to be able to engage in authentic teaching and learning in your classroom? Why?
3. What can you do to get to know your student's history of reading and literacy?
4. Which of these strategies of getting to know your students is one that you use, want to use, or want to expand in your classroom? What are steps you can take to get to know your students to begin to use these strategies?

Chapter 3
The LEAP Framework for Inclusive Texts

Framework

There are ways to be actionable in transforming and changing the world of education in order to help cultivate, uplift, and grow students who are accepting, empathetic, thoughtful, and compassionate, as well as culturally competent and aware. For us to be able to teach students to cultivate these qualities, we must begin with ourselves.

When we begin with ourselves, we can begin to create a shift in the world, in our schools, and in our school communities. We can then pour into the children who are going to be changemakers, future leaders, thinkers, doers, teachers of the world in which we live. We can pour into the teachers who lead our students. We can pour into their families and their communities. The idea of pouring into individuals is the teaching and learning that happens in schools. Reading outside of each of our bubbles is part of that essential work. Taking the necessary steps to move from being in our own bubbles to expanding outside of them needs to happen for our children to become empathetic, compassionate, and curious adults who know and do better than the generations that have come before them. It needs to happen for us as well to get regrounded in those qualities.

We have seen on the news time and time again where students all over the world are leading the charge and the nation through their actions. We are seeing instances where they are speaking up for human rights. We are seeing where students aren't afraid to be the changemakers that our world needs. They aren't afraid of being the ones who shake the nation's moral compasses. I suspect they are doing this because they see how they can change the world by using their voices and taking action.

These students did not become action takers overnight. These revolutionary acts were cultivated. Someone or many someones have poured their learning into them and have taught them ways to use their voices to speak out against injustice. Seeing the ways in which they are speaking out, I believe it because they have taken the time to read, learn, grow, and expand their bubbles. They have taken time to listen and learn from the stories of others. I am sure along their learning journeys that they have had great leaders, mentors, and teachers who have shepherded them through their learning. They have learned what equity looks, sounds, and feels like, and they can imagine what it looks, sounds, and feels like when things are inequitable. Some of these students have learned to know what it means to have things undeniably accessible to you, and they can also look around and see when things aren't accessible to others.

These action-takers can observe, acknowledge, and speak out when they see injustice done to others who may or may not look like or have the same identity markers as them. They are able to do this because they are grounded in learning, and that learning is grounded in purpose. Their learning and purpose have now extended far beyond reading a book or text in a classroom and far beyond discussing it in a group. That is possibly where their learning took root; however, they have sprouted that learning. They have moved from that rooting of learning and growing to action—although the learning never stops. They know that and so do we. However, they are taking the learning that they have absorbed into actionable steps to be better people in this world. They have taken that learning into practice. That is the next step when you are expanding your bookshelves and becoming not just a learner or expander of your bubble but an activator of it. I call this type of learning the *learning ladder* for students, which includes adults too.

Let's think about how these students' voices were cultivated. Where did they get their courage, the cultivation of their voices, and their tenacity? I believe it starts in the classroom, whether the classroom is your home or your school. It starts with their knowledge, their experiences, their life learning growing up—all of it. That learning and knowledge continue with them being actionable and that learning begins with teachers. When I say teachers, I mean the teachers in their homes—their families, their caregivers, loved ones—teaching them before they even step foot into the classroom. Then another layer is added—their teachers in school. The teachers are the ones who are with them in school after the age of five or so. The student's/action taker's learning/advocacy can either start or continue there, in those spaces. The learning that takes place here is through a teacher who has a deep understanding of culturally responsive teaching where, intertwined in their teaching, are providing spaces for voices to be lifted. But in contrast, these voices could also be cultivated through the absence of that support. Either way, these are the voices of young people that you hear taking a stand for human rights today. These are the voices of those who look like them or don't look like them. These are the voices of those who may have the same identity markers and may not. The voices of these action-takers either begins and/or continues with learning. And that learning starts from somewhere.

The Learning Ladder

The learning ladder is a concept that I have adapted from the NTL Institute of Applied Behavioral Science Learning Pyramid which correlates with the L portion—the learning portion—of the LEAP framework. There are nine steps in the learning ladder: observing/listening, life experiences, individual reading and learning, reading and learning with others, discussing with others, using your voice, showing actions, speaking out to teach others, and making change in the world. Figure 3.1 shows each of the steps to the learning ladder. All learning begins with observation, listening, and experiences; however, as we take each step, our learning journey may look different for each of us.

Although this is called a ladder, making change is fluid, and the steps can be intertwined and returned to when needed. In other words, you can step up and/or step back down the ladder. That is what active learners do. Active learners learn to have discernment when a shift up or down the ladder needs to take place. Until that learning of discernment takes hold, the teacher is the facilitator in the movement on the ladder. Sometimes that teacher is within—the little voice that may whisper to you that change needs to happen. Some of us may hear that voice louder than others, but it's there. Let's dig into the various steps on the learning ladder.

Observing/Listening

In this step of the learning, the learner is taking in learning through all their senses. They are taking time to observe and listen. This can happen at any step of the ladder. Learning happens when you take time to slow down and take the learning in. You can observe in a multitude of ways but mostly through

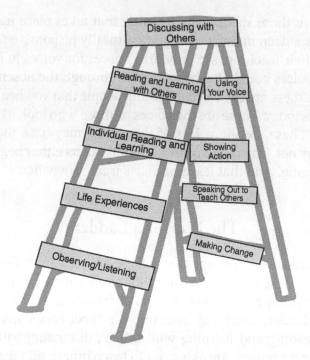

Figure 3.1   Steps on the learning ladder
SOURCE: Adapted from the NTL Institute of Applied Behavioral Science Learning Pyramid

observation and actively listening. In this step you can be observing and listening in your own bubble while simultaneously expanding your bubble. Observing and listening is an important step on the learning ladder. We must be humble enough and open enough to take this critical step. For example, in school, I wasn't taught about life of Black people before they were enslaved. I was not given the history of my ancestors prior to them being unwillingly captured in chains and brought to America. I was in the observing and listening stage to what was being taught. I was in the observing and listening stage to what was not being taught as well. However, the curiosity within always had me asking the question, "Where were Black folks prior to this horrific point in history of enslavement?" Although I did not have many teachers prior to middle school who taught through culturally responsive pedagogy, the curiosity within drove me to want to learn more.

Life Experiences

Throughout life, it is inevitable that life experiences will impact your learning. Life experiences are important to every single human, and they craft what we believe and the way we move in the world, as well as crafting the way we think about the world. Life experiences can be powerful forces in what we believe. They are something that we will always have and will forever be part of our journey. However, sometimes what we grow to believe and continue learning throughout life may not serve us well as we expand our worlds and our beliefs and in our learning, we craft new beliefs. Let me bring us back to the example of my learning about life of Black folks prior to enslavement. My curiosity along with life experiences created in me a drive for learning about my bubble, my people, and my ancestors who weren't written in the story—I was learning HIS-story, but not THE story. As I moved throughout school, I realized that I had to create my own learning here—and read for myself.

Individual Reading and Learning

Reading and learning happens throughout life. We usually begin by reading and learning about ourselves, including who we are, how we identify, and what our cultures and heritage are—our own bubbles. Depending on how you identify, your individual learning and reading may look different from others. However, when you are open to the expansion of your bubbles through inclusive literature, individual reading and learning begins to open the mind to lived experiences outside of your world—outside of your bubble. We can make the choice to begin learning and expanding our bubbles even more as we take in more learning. In this step the learning is happening individually. For me, as I began taking on this learning, I began to look for articles and books about Black people living before enslavement. I came across Mansa Musa—the richest Black person in the world and ruler of Mali. He believed in academics, was grounded in faith, and built his community. This learning filled my soul and expanded my own bubble. I had to do this learning for myself because it didn't happen through my teachers in school. I had to do my own reading and learning.

Reading and Learning with Others

Reading and learning with others helps expand your bubble even more. This learning is taken to another level when you can read and learn alongside others.

It is important and effective during this step in learning to read and learn alongside others who may have different identity markers than you. In doing this, especially when you are learning alongside folks of marginalized communities, it will be important that you take a listening stance. In this learning step, affinity groups are also incredibly helpful in the learning journey.

Affinity groups, also known as identity-based groups, can have a great impact on learning. These groups provide a supportive place for dialogue, validation, and help to empower its members. When you can read and learn from others, you are able to listen and learn from others, and others can listen and learn from you. This helps to promote connection and build community while learning. As I continued my learning of Mansa Musa, I also began sharing my learning with others in my community. Some already knew about him and for others it was new information. We began discussing about the why behind hiding this information in schools. We discussed the reasoning, emotions that came up for us, and what now. Learning alongside others is a way to build community while learning. It can be a refreshing space.

Discussing with Others

Taking reading and learning into in-depth discussion allows you to move learning to a whole other level. This is where important conversations take place—sometimes what may feel like hard conversations. This step is where you can truly begin to build compassion and empathy. It will be important to ensure that trust and psychological safety are present when you begin opening and sharing learning or unlearning. During this step it is also important that you establish agreements during the discussions. We want to ensure that we aren't harming others in the discussion process. As I moved from discussing in community with affinity groups to outside of those spaces, I had to ensure that trust was present and that I felt safe enough to discuss and share my learning. I had to know that I was in a space where I would be heard and listened to. I discussed with folks that I knew also wanted to learn and unlearn. I felt safe enough and engaged in thoughtful discussion. We not only discussed the amazing history of Mansa Musa, but the why behind not learning his story or others prior to now. This discussion helped to create more awareness and spark our fire to moving into another step of the learning ladder to use my voice even more.

Using Your Voice

Using your voice as you read and learn—individually and with others—is one way to internalize your learning. As you learn, it is important to share your learning that may benefit others inside and outside of your bubble. When you can begin to share your learning and infuse what you have learned into your day-to-day lived experiences with others, it can be impactful. When learning can move into the step on the ladder of using your voice, this is where cultivating change or planting a seed can happen. Using your voice can mean in spaces outside of what may be comfortable for you. Push past that discomfort while also being aware that in using your voice, sometimes you may get it wrong. Sometimes you may use your voice in times and places when your voice isn't warranted, or you may say or do something harmful to others. When and if that occurs, take time to reflect, acknowledge the harm done, authentically apologize, and dig back into the work of re-learning and unlearning for yourself and others. There may be times, especially if you identify in the margins of society, that using your voice may cause harm to you. Where sharing truth provokes harm on you so much so that you may have to take time in your own bubble to heal and be in community with those you feel safe with. Ultimately, make sure that you take care of your well-being. There have been times in my journey where I have been harmed in the process of using my voice. This happened out of ignorance of the other party, but also because I was trying to do this work in silos. Therefore, I felt broken down and defeated. Being in a community with others is a key component of the learning journey.

Showing Action

Showing action moves from *actually* using your voice to doing something, which could be attending school-board meetings to fight against book ban policies that are put in place in schools, attending a local county-wide meeting, or creating or adding banned books in a Little Free Library in your neighborhood. It could be teaching from diverse perspectives and using books to teach truth. It can be as big as speaking up and being an ally or it could be standing with others who are speaking up. It could be making a plan about the need for inclusive and diverse texts in your learning community. Connecting learnings in your reading to the world today and then doing something about it is showing action. Ask yourself, what can I do, even if it seems small, to make the world better for us all?

Teaching Others

When you show action and then begin to teach others what you have learned from your reading or even lived experiences, you begin to expand your learning to others. You have shifted the learning from learning within to learning that can move outward. This could look like teaching your students about the Indigenous People who live in the rainforest that you are learning about in science. The learning can be in connection with colonialism and what that means for stolen land. Teaching others can be the students in your classroom, the teachers in your building, teachers on your team, or it can be family at Thanksgiving Dinner. It can be in those moments where you see the curiosity or ignorance of others that open that door of teaching. This is where you are continually planting seeds. You may not see the seeds sprout right away; however, you realize the power of using your voice to begin to create change even when you cannot see it. For instance, I shared my learning with other teachers in my teacher team about the great and wealthy, Mansa Musa. In teaching teachers in my teacher team about Mansa Musa and his life before enslavement, they were appreciative of the learning. I planted a seed of curiosity that maybe, just maybe, other Black students in their classes may have the same question—where were my people before enslavement? That simple question rooted in curiosity is the little sprout for the change we need.

Making Change

The idea of making change can feel daunting. When we initially think about making change, we think of the big-picture change that we want to see happen right now. We want to see a huge shift in our world and then magically, poof, we end racism, sexism, capitalism, misogyny, and homophobia. Unfortunately, it's not that easy. But what if we look at making change as something we do in our learning communities, the communities that we live in, our own bubbles? Making change can be big or small—but making change is something. It could be a shift in beliefs or in someone's thinking by a discussion that took place or a question that was asked. It could be a change from within and in our own thought process that can have an impact on others.

The learning ladder is not a perfect ladder as you learn to move in this world as a better human. There are probably spaces and steps on the ladder that were missed; however, the ladder is rooted in learning and learning on purpose and with purpose to ultimately move toward growth and change.

The LEAP Framework

When the short-lived reckoning happened in 2020 after the heartbreaking, unnecessary, and unlawful murder of George Floyd, there were lots of folks who seemed to want to learn and grow. Not that this was the first brutal murder of a Black man or woman by the hands of a police officer, but due to technology and social media, it was a moment where we were all able to see for ourselves the moments before and after the death of George Floyd.

It was heartbreaking. The humans who decided to watch the videos most likely couldn't watch without overwhelming feelings of sadness, grief, and maybe even guilt. After this incident was aired, a great deal of folks of all races wanted to learn more about racism and injustice. They wanted to learn and enter a space of perspective-taking, empathy, and change. Black squares flooded social media feeds, books by Black authors were flying off the shelves, and folks were speaking out against racism and police brutality like never before. It felt like maybe, just maybe, the murder of George Floyd was not in vain and that this time was a time of change—real change, sustainable change.

That's how it felt for me, anyway. I had hope and I held onto it. During this time, book sales about race increased up to 6,800%, illustrating the role that anti-racism literature played in the country's "cultural reckoning" (Forbes, 2020). However, it was short-lived. My hope became deflated and unfortunately, sales of books on racism, on the history of racism, and on how to be a better ally have significantly declined since 2020. Literary agents say that publishers' appetite for books that examine race and racism has dwindled. Book bans and the politicization of human rights, anti-racism and just being a good human, may have something to do with that. Whatever the reason, in 2020 our nation wanted to ensure that we took the time to learn. Learn more about the history of racism in the United States and what got us to this place.

People were seeking the truth in our history instead of watered-down versions of history. During this time, it seemed that folks were opening up more, talking more, and listening more. I would be remiss if I didn't say that the racism and injustice faced by Black and Brown folks isn't something we can just learn when about it tickles our fancy, because Black and Brown folks can't just pause those experiences—we don't hold that privilege; it is something we live every day. However, during that time folks were more open than they ever had been to learning and being better allies.

In doing so, their learning began with a listening stance. They took time to listen to others that are identified as BIPOC. They observed and listened—they were on the first step of the learning ladder, and reading was how they jump-started their education during this time. In fact, reading is often a starting place when people want to learn about themselves and expand their bubbles to learn about others, too.

This type of learning stance is where we must begin as students (as we all are students—learning to be better). When thinking about the teaching for ourselves and for our students, let's take time to visualize what that learning could look like. Let's visualize getting to that place—the place of learning and growing. The place that can truly guide us to be better learners of inclusive texts and teachers of inclusive texts so that we expand not only our bubbles but the bubbles of our students. This is the starting place for the LEAP framework, which is essential in reading outside your bubbles. It is a framework that educators can use when reading outside our bubbles to expand to grow into learners and teachers who can read and think critically and participate in thoughtful discourse. This is a framework we can use to ensure that we have access to and use inclusive texts when teaching the students in our classrooms. This framework is one where equity is always at the forefront of your mind. Whether you are a teacher in a school building, online, or a teacher in the home, or a parent, using the LEAP framework will help you to read outside your bubbles, expand your bookshelf, and intentionally teach outside your bubbles for the overall well-being of your students. Figure 3.2 shows the cornerstones of the LEAP framework.

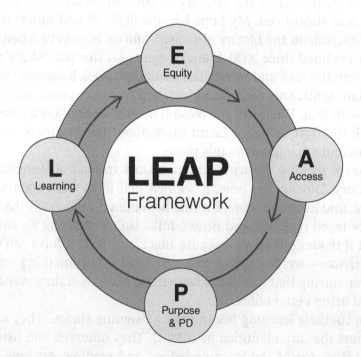

Figure 3.2 The LEAP framework

Learning using the LEAP Framework

Making the decision to be a learner is a powerful choice that opens doors to personal growth, skill development, and lifelong fulfillment that helps to create an environment for learning. It shows an overall commitment to growth for yourself and for your students. It is like an ongoing professional learning community within. The community begins with you—but continues to others—as you begin to share your learning with others. It takes a level of openness and curiosity to be in a state of learning. The openness is a part of self that knows there is always more to be learned. It comes from the part of yourself that knows that this world could be better if everyone takes a step toward being better each and every day.

I would describe myself as a forever learner. I will also say that some parts of learning, depending on what it is, can be uncomfortable, uneasy, and unsettling. Sometimes learning doesn't always feel like excitement and pleasure. And that is okay. For me, as a Black woman, it is hard to hear about history that I didn't know about as a child—the history that I didn't learn in school. History can be painful and heart-wrenching, and history can be enlightening and empowering. However, it is history that can help me learn more. I can learn more about myself, my ancestors, my culture, my lineage—I can also learn more about others, their ancestors, their cultures.

Even though I have a lot of varying emotions when it comes to learning, I still take a learning stance, because I want us as a society, as a culture, to be better for ourselves, for each other, and for the next generation looking at us as models. So yes, learning needs to happen. We need to be able and open to be learners for ourselves and learners for the students that we serve each and every day because the kids are watching.

What Learning Looks Like Inside and Outside of Schools

I know that educators have state standards that they must teach your students. I want you to think about those standards for English and language arts, science, social studies, even math. Think about the standards and evaluate whose stories are missing. Whose stories do I need to learn about to get to the whole history and not just one perspective? Whose stories do my students need to know about and haven't been learning about? Those are two questions you should continuously ask yourself as a learner and educator of students. You also need to think of learning, especially when reading outside of your bubble, as mirrors, windows, and sliding-glass doors.

The concept of mirrors, windows, and sliding-glass doors was coined by Dr. Rudine Sims Bishop in her article entitled "Mirrors, Windows, and Sliding Glass Doors" in 1990. Bishop stated, "Books are sometimes *windows*, offering views of worlds that may be real or imagined, familiar or strange. These windows are also *sliding-glass doors*, and readers have only to walk through in imagination to become part of whatever world has been created or recreated by the author. When lighting conditions are just right, however, a window can also be a *mirror*."

I will talk about these concepts extensively in the next few chapters as we move through the L portion of LEAP; however, mirrors, windows, and sliding-glass doors help a reader and learner to cultivate self-compassion, compassion for others, empathy, and perspective-taking. As you read and learn, allow yourself to open your mind and your heart and get super curious. You can learn from books, articles, credible historians, credible sources online, well-known voices on social media, and stories from folks who are from the communities that you need and want to learn from. We are grounding our learning from a state of open-mindedness and curiosity. This curiosity begins with self; however, the more we become curious learners as teachers, the better teachers and facilitators of learning we are for our students.

For example, when I taught World War II to fifth graders, I took time to think about the various perspectives during that time period—before, during, and after the war. There are varying perspectives from the different countries involved in that war such as France, Germany, Great Britain, and America. But even when thinking about the American perspective, I was curious about how folks from different races and cultures perceived the war during that time period. As I planned for this unit, I got super curious and wanted to offer my students varying perspectives as I taught these lessons. That meant I had to do some learning for myself before planning and teaching my students. I took a learner's stance while creating and building out these lessons about World War II.

You know what happened? I got really excited to be able to teach my students this unit, and I was excited to learn and to be able to offer a variety of stories and perspectives during this time period. But I didn't want to allow my excitement to overshadow the curiosity and learning that I wanted my students to learn to do for themselves. I wanted them to expand their own curiosity and perspective in the process. Just as we, as educators, get really curious about the standards, we want our students to have that same curiosity and critical thinking in their learning. We want them to engage in learning in the same way. We must teach that level of questioning, model that level of questioning, and take time to share our thinking, our questioning, with our students. It takes being a learner and being vulnerable to share our own process in our learning. It takes being a learner for ourselves and for our students. It takes reading outside our bubbles and modeling that learning in front of our students in very intentional ways for them to see that learning never ends—the teacher is always the student. Wanting to be better and do better doesn't end. Even as we learn prepare our lessons, our learning continues. It continues with equitable conditions in education in place in order to get to the learning that one so desires.

Equity: What Does Equity Have to Do with the LEAP Framework?

According to the National Equity Project, "Educational equity means that each child receives what they need to develop to their full academic and social potential." There are many places and spaces that say they are doing the work of equity but do not even want to use the word "equity" as it relates to students, their classrooms, or their environments. The word "equity" is banned from use in some districts and some professional learning environments. How can you say that you want the best for all students and not think about what is equitable?

The action of educational equity should be threaded into each and every conversation in education. I am not talking about using the word and not doing the work, and I am not talking about equality. Equality does not make schools and school environments an equal playing ground for every single student. What one student, one school, or even one entire school district may need is entirely different from the next. Context matters. History matters. Therefore, that is where the word "equity" and the action behind the word come into play.

We must make the learning equitable for students, and that means learning at a high level with high expectations. That means having teachers who have the skills and knowledge necessary to teach all students at high levels. It means ensuring that students have what they need each and every day, while realizing that their needs will vary from student to student and school to school and year to year. It means looking at discrepancies in data when thinking about harsh discipline practices for Black boys and Black girls. It also means making sure that when researching and contemplating curriculum for the classroom—specifically reading curriculum—that the reading that students have access to create mirrors, windows, and sliding glass doors. It means taking the time to intentionally and purposely have students read inside and outside of their bubbles. It also means intentionally, purposely, and consistently looking at the education system through an equity lens. This will allow you to see barriers, invisibility, and hindrances in the learning system—and do what needs to be done to alter them. This means finding pathways in a broken system to give our students what they need to learn, grow, and thrive.

Accessibility: Do Students Have Access?

Accessibility is the third step in the LEAP framework. Although accessibility can be intertwined throughout the framework, keeping access top of mind is always pertinent. Ensuring that students, teachers, leaders, and the community have access to inclusive text is pivotal in making sure that the resources needed are there for the use of all.

Making sure inclusive texts are integrated into daily lessons needs to be a classroom-wide, school-wide, and county-wide goal for all. Once that is a goal for all, then ensuring that stakeholders have access to those texts should be a priority. This means that professional learning is accessible to all educators to learn the best strategies to teach educators how to effectively integrate inclusive texts into their lessons and learn about culturally responsive pedagogy. That professional learning should be placed in the budget for all teachers.

The budget of a school shows what is valuable and that value should be in the learning of educators and students. It only takes one voice to begin these pivotal discussions about the importance of equity and access in your learning community. These discussions can lead to important transformation in your communities. That one voice could be yours. Educators often feel that their voice isn't heard or as though if they use their voices, it won't change anything, but it will, especially if you come up with a plan. If you see a gap in your school community's accessibility, find spaces for solutions. The solution might not be perfect, or completely fleshed out, but it is a start. Access is critical. Without access to the inclusive, diverse literature for our students, teachers, and leaders, how can we do this good work of transforming the world into one step, one voice, and one community at a time? We need to make sure that we have access to what we need, and that may look different in different schools and communities.

Purpose and Professional Learning in the LEAP Framework

As I continued using the LEAP framework in the work I do, I began to really dive into the last P. As I began to think about the individual or collaborative learning that takes place in the L portion of the framework, I initially honed in on the professional learning that needs to take place in the entire community. Of course, together as a team we all need professional learning to align on our goals. But with the alignment of our goals, we need to take time to establish and ground in purpose.

In other words, as a collective, in the communities that we are teaching, instructing, and leading in, we need to ensure that we have the sure footing of what our purpose is and the *why* behind reading outside our bubbles—the *why* behind what makes it important to read outside our bubbles and what makes it important for the next generation to do so as well. Once the purpose is clear for the community in which you are serving, then the professional learning can take place. Together as a community, you can dive into the what and the how in reading outside the bubbles that surround each and every one of us and begin to change a system—to shake it up—to create the change that we desire for our students, a change we desire for us.

Take the LEAP

We will take a deep dive into the LEAP framework in the following chapters. It is one that begins and ends with learning and is grounded in purpose. To do this impactful and much-needed work of reading outside of your bubble, you must be a learner with an open mind. This framework is one that is heart work. It is the work of being a change agent in schools, in your communities, and in yourselves. With this framework, we can make sure that all students are seen and valued, have a sense of belonging, and have what they need to learn at their greatest potential in order for them to thrive.

This LEAP framework is for students to be able to showcase their geniuses because they have seen others who have come before them showcase theirs. Taking the leap is infusing the LEAP framework into our curriculum in actionable ways. Curriculum is where the power lies. Bettina Love says in her book *Punished for Dreaming* that curriculum is one of the most powerful tools in education to teach all children that people like them and people from whom they are different are beautiful, powerful, and valuable, and so were their ancestors (Love, 2023).

Curriculum becomes powerful when our students can see themselves within it—all of our children. We want our students to be able to hold a mirror in front of themselves and say, "I can learn and thrive because others like me have learned and thrived."

Let's Reflect

1. As you learn inside and outside your bubble, take time to think about where you are on the learning ladder. Take time to reflect on what it takes to get to another step on the ladder. What does that look, sound, and feel like?

2. As you learn about the LEAP framework, is there a certain step in the framework that you feel is an area of strength? Is there a step in the framework that is an area of growth?

3. What emotions come up for you as you read through this chapter? Take time to reflect on your emotions and their root cause.

Chapter 4
Learning: Seeing Mirrors with Inclusive Text

Learn

Before you can begin reading outside of your bubble, it is important for you to really get to know your own bubble—yourself. That means taking some time on the listening, observing steps of the learning ladder. It is important for you to be able to take time to really deeply reflect on who you are, including your culture, your race, your family—and what that looks and sounds like in your life. This is where you take in and reflect on life experiences as well.

This is no different for children. It is important that children know themselves or start getting to know themselves. Obviously, as children grow, they change—just as we do as adults. However, in knowing yourself and where you come from, you learn to see yourself or versions of who you are represented. It is important for you to see mirrors in various aspects of your life. This representation is important in your personal life, your community, your school, and places you are a part of because when representation is present you are able to see parts of yourself. This representation is called a *mirror*. A mirror is a representation of a place on the learning ladder where you can look and see yourself or a version of yourself. Books are a great place for one to begin seeing mirrors. Even as a baby, when you are being read to by your loved ones, it is important that you see yourself in the pages of the book. Think about that very last page in many board books designed for babies: There is often a physical mirror for babies to see themselves. It is no different as those babies grow. We want them to have those mirrors, threaded throughout the book. We want them to see versions of themselves and be able to connect. Let's take time to look at what a mirror might show us.

Let's Visualize

Imagine you are looking into a mirror. As you look into the mirror, you don't see yourself at all. You see someone else. You know it is not you reflecting back at you, but it is someone else. Now ask yourself what you really see in that mirror . . . rather who do you see? Once you do that, I want you to rewind the hands of time into your classroom as a child. It could be any grade or age, preferably in elementary school, but it could be middle or high school as well. Think about the types of books that were introduced to you as a student. Go *really* deep here. I want you to scan the shelves in your school library. Imagine yourself walking up and down the aisles looking for your allotted two books to check out. I am sure as you are going back in time, visualizing, you are getting excited about the books that bring you memories of (I hope) a joyful experience of being exposed to books. Some funny books, some sad books, some books that connected to your life. This is natural. There may be books that really did it for you, the books that made you fall in love with reading. There may be some books that made you dislike reading as well. I want to honor both experiences.

When I think about my visualization, I begin to really wonder and dig deep into curiosity. I think about the books that were in my school library. I think about the books that were read aloud to me. I know that Dr. Seuss' books were in the pile, along with *Wayside School Is Falling Down* by Louis Sachar, *Miss Nelson is Missing* by Harry Allard, and *A Light in the Attic* by Shel Silverstein. Now most of these books I absolutely loved and still do (aside from Seuss, as I mentioned). I loved being read to and began to truly love reading in about the fifth grade.

But honestly, as I scanned the shelves in my visualization, there were not many books on the shelves that I saw myself in. There weren't a ton of covers of Black girls on the shelves of the library. There weren't a ton of Black families on the cover or even a Black teacher—like Miss Nelson in *Miss Nelson Is Missing*. Gasp! Does this mean that in the 1980s there weren't Black authors writing children's books about Black folks? No; however, these books were not presented to most children—at least not at the school I attended. I went to school with children who came from many cultures and backgrounds. So why wasn't I able to see myself in books? Why weren't other students able to do the same? It is because there weren't tons of folks in my school who were intentional about putting these books that gave us mirrors on the shelves. There were not many adults in the building who knew or took the time to think about just how important it is to have these mirrors for children.

The Importance of Mirrors

If students cannot see themselves represented in books, how can they truly see others? When I say the words "see" themselves, I am talking about students being able to have folks who look like them in books, not just in the storylines but on the covers. Seeing yourself is also being able to read about similar experiences that you have encountered in your life. Seeing yourself is being able to identify with stories, histories, and characters in books. The students who usually struggle to find mirrors are students who come from marginalized communities. Students who are Black, Indigenous, and children of color are the ones who sometimes struggle to find that mirror. I am also talking about students who identify as nonbinary or transgender. I am talking about students who may have a family that may look different from a "traditional" family structure. When I was in school, the books that I was presented with were books of the white majority. They were stories about white families, history from the dominant perspective, and white people living their lives.

Around second grade, my mother brought home a book from the school book fair where she taught physical education at the elementary school called *The People Could Fly* by Virginia Hamilton that included folktales about enslaved Africans, which included animal tales, fairy tales, and supernatural tales.

Although I enjoyed reading the tales, I desired to read more books about my life as a Black child written by authors who were also Black. Although there were not many books that showed Black people living in the late 1980s, there were some books that I read that I did find some connection to. For instance, I read The Baby-Sitters Club series by Ann M. Martin, published in 1986, I was in fourth grade. As I read, I realized that Jessi was Black, and Claudia was Japanese. I was hooked!

At the time, I didn't realize these were the reasons I was hooked onto this series of books, but I know now as an adult that this was where my shift took place in my reading engagement. I began to look at books differently. I began to see that I, too, could be a character in the story—even if it wasn't the main character. I saw that my story, like Jessi's, was important enough to be featured in a book. It gave me a real connection to the character and maximized my reading engagement. It made me want to read and read and read. In fact, it made me curious about books and what books meant to me as a student—and what that meant for me as a Black student.

The Reflection of Mirrors
Cultivate Engagement

Curiosity is what helps students want to read. It helps to cultivate the reading engagement that teachers often long for in their classrooms. That engagement must begin somewhere. Even before a child begins to learn to read, curiosity is the driving force for students wanting to learn. So how do we foster reading engagement in students? How do we make sure that students are curious?

We must read books to students that create the mirror experience so their curiosity increases the desire to read. Books should be a reflection of themselves so they can connect with books on a deeper level. It becomes a sense of self-affirmation—a place where they can see their own experiences as a part of the overall experience of being human. However, if most books favor only whiteness or exhibit what we have been socialized to believe is the "right" way to be in society, it gives marginalized students the message that they don't belong, that one story is more important than the other, and/or that their stories don't matter. Although this may not be the intent, it is how the lack of inclusivity impacts the students we serve. It is the overall negative effect that our students of marginalized communities internalize by not being part of a book to choose on the bookshelf time and time again. But when the student can connect to the book on a self-affirmational level, the active reading component becomes ignited. The reader has now moved from reading in a passive way to reading in a more active and responsive way. When this happens, the teacher sees the students reading more, talking about the text more, and being excited about the book that is being read. This type of engagement really becomes a placeholder in the reader's mind, and that connection cannot be undone.

Think about the book that really did it for you, when your whole reading engagement was turned around. It might have been a book you read in elementary, middle, high school, or beyond, but most people remember the books—or the series of books—that took their reading to the next level. Or maybe even had them look at where reading has a place in their life. Most people can remember the name of the book, where they were in life, and what the book was about. Connection cultivates engagement. Now I do realize that there is a lot more that needs to take place before a student is fully committed to reading or being read to; however, if there isn't a connection to the text, it is less likely you will engage your readers in activity—they will be passive readers but rarely active readers.

Cultivating Active Readers

Passive reading happens when a person is reading but not engaged. They may read the words but don't comprehend what they are saying. Passive readers may even understand what the text is saying; however, they haven't engaged enough in the text to find themes or purpose of the text being read. They may fall asleep while reading or even being read to due to lack of engagement in the text. If any of this has happened to you while reading or being read to, you were being a passive reader.

When you think about students who struggle to be active readers, what comes to mind? Is it a lack of interest in the text? Is there a lack of relevance to their lives? What if the reason that the students struggle to become active readers is because of missing mirrors in the text? What if it is because from the start of engaging with a book—from the cover, to reading the summary of the book, and even how the author identifies—there is already a lack of interest? Now, there will not always be a classroom where every book that is read by students or being read to students will be a book that centers only on folks of marginalized communities. However, teachers should prioritize creating inclusive bubbles, or environments, for all students who are part of the classroom. Even if the students in the classroom are predominantly white and most students come from a "middle-class" household, it is still important to read books that represent inclusive bubbles. This helps kids to learn the world that they are a part of—what the world looks like, sounds like, and feels like. That means including books on the shelves that students can see themselves in. That means having books that are written by and illustrated by folks of the global majority. That means having folks from marginalized communities tell the stories that the students will find relevant, whether they are fiction or nonfiction. This is how you can create active readers: by cultivating and celebrating an inclusive environment. That means creating a bubble where everyone can look in the mirror and see themselves, their family, their lived experiences, their history, and their present—where self-affirmation is at the core. Let's dig into ways that this can happen when we are intentional about making this an ongoing reality for all students.

Creating an Inclusive Environment

Being intentional about creating the environment where all students feel seen, heard, and valued is the single most important foundation that an educator and school can give students. Once students know that you want this for them—once they know that you care about who they are, how they identify, and how they value the experiences they bring into the educational space—that child will be able to truly thrive in their learning journey because they can bring who they are to the space—who they really are. The environment should be created with students at the core. Let's get into how you can do that.

Before students enter the classroom, think about how you want them to feel as they enter the room—their learning community. Imagine the students arriving and quietly moving about the room and looking at the walls, the materials for learning, the shelves. What do you want them to see?

Do you want to know what I would want my students to see? As they walked around my room, I would want them to see real pictures of students reading and engaging in learning on the walls. I would want them to see students from all different cultures and races in those pictures. As they continued to walk around, I would want them to see the materials that were prepared for them to learn. In my classroom, they would see construction papers in all different colors including beautiful shades of the colors of one's skin. They would see crayons or colored pencils that were vibrant in colors that they could imagine themselves using. They would see the beautiful range of flesh-colored crayons or colored pencils that they could use to draw and color themselves.

As the students walked to the bookshelves, they would see books—so many books, no matter what subject that is being taught—that showed *them* in the stories, whether fiction or nonfiction. Even if I taught math in a middle or high school setting, students would see books about mathematicians from all races, cultures, nationalities, and genders, including nonbinary. They would see both fiction and nonfiction books that included the theme or touchpoint of what we were studying in the books in our room. They would see the mirrors they needed in order to see themselves in history, to see themselves in the present, and to see themselves in the possibility of the future. These books would be displayed loudly and proudly in the room—*our* room.

Why? Because as a student enters the room, they can look around and see what you deem as important to you as an educator in teaching them and for them as your student learning. The visualization that I just took you through is the result of intentionality in what I want students to see and feel as they enter their learning environment. This learning environment also includes you, the educator, because you are always a learner, even if you are learning from your students (especially when you are learning from your students!). However, we the educators create the conditions for this learning to take place. That is where the intentionality lies. As the learning begins and students begin to enter the room to learn, then you would also see the evidence of their learning and genius on the walls of my classroom. That is also a way to create inclusive learning spaces. But that space must first be prepared, and that takes work. The good work is when you know what amount of genius is about to happen because you set the students up to thrive even before they step foot in your classroom.

The Good Work: Securing Books with Mirrors

Books are expensive. If you have ever spoken to a new teacher who just graduated from college or even think back to when you got your first job as a teacher, you might remember how much money you felt like you had to pour into your classroom. Especially now, with all of these "Pinterest-worthy" classrooms, you might feel as if you have to make your space ready for social media. Welcoming and inclusive, yes, but social media worthy, no.

Still, it can get expensive to buy the items you need for your classroom so that it is an inclusive and welcoming space. I won't get on my soapbox yet about how I think teachers should be getting paid so much more and that classroom materials such as books, pencils, construction paper, lined paper, tissues, and hand sanitizer should not be coming out of their own pockets. However, there are some schools that have classroom libraries for their teachers, and the school library is also a great way to use the library books in your classroom until you build your own classroom library.

But let's talk about a couple of ways to get books in your room.

- The First Book Marketplace organization's focus is on getting inclusive texts into the classroom at cheaper rates. It is a wonderful organization to begin building your library where students feel seen and include mirrors for them. This is one way to get these books on your shelves at a discounted rate.
- Retired teachers or teachers who are about to retire are gold. However, I will say this, and this is very important: You must take time to vet the books you place on your shelves. Some books might not be relevant.
- Facebook Marketplace and eBay are also a great way to get books into your classroom. Teachers often sell items on here and those items are often books.
- Writing grants can help to get books into your classrooms. You can write a grant through DonorsChoose. I would definitely keep a grant ready to go on that site, because you never know when a company may want to send the items from the grant.

- Amazon Wishlist is a handy list to ask family, friends, and folks in your community to help with your classroom library.
- The local library is another great way to get books into your classrooms. Make sure you have a library card, so you have access to the books there. Usually for teachers they have an unlimited number of books to get. When you go, make sure you bring your travel wagon to transport them.

As you move through these ways of getting books in your classroom for curriculum use and student use, let's take some time to talk about how to vet books.

Vetting Inclusive Texts for Your Shelves

We must be intentional about the books that we put on our shelves so that we can create mirrors, windows, and sliding-glass doors for our students. That means we must take time to really analyze the books we place on the shelves for our students to read as well as the ones that we read to them. This takes a lot of time and purposeful close reading at the beginning, especially if this is new to you; however, the more you begin building the lenses for vetting these books, the easier it will be. According to Joy Shioshita, writer of the reprint in this Lee and Low article entitled, *"Beyond Good Intention: Selecting Multicultural Literature,"* There are 10 ways to vet books before putting them on your bookshelves for students:

1. **Check the Cover of the Book:** Make sure the cover of the book doesn't have insulting illustrations and stereotypes of the marginalized communities that the book may be about. For example, is the illustration on the cover showing Indigenous Peoples as "savages." We often bypass the cover without looking at the cover with intention.
2. **Check the Illustrations in the Book:** As you look at the illustrations in the book, just as you would the cover, make sure that the illustrations aren't insulting to the marginalized communities the book is centering on and that there aren't stereotypes depicted in the illustrations. An example here would be illustrations of racist caricatures of members of the Asian community. That is what I saw on the pages of Dr. Seuss' books. It is disheartening to see. Make sure you look through the pages of the book with open eyes.
3. **Look at the Accuracy of the Text:** Make sure you ensure the accuracy of the information in the book. Sometimes books from veteran teachers who may have not vetted their books in a while may have to be checked. Also, there are some books being currently printed that do not have accurate information in them.

4. **Look for Stereotypes:** This one is also important. Folks from marginalized communities aren't monoliths. Be careful that the books on your shelves don't reinforce negative stereotypes. Authors shouldn't be assigning character traits or personality traits to a whole group of people. This also applies to the setting of books. Keep in mind stereotypes about where people of marginalized communities or underprivileged live.

5. **Look for Offensive Words Used to Insult an Entire Race, Ethnicity, or Identity:** Some words in the text can be loaded and have insulting overtones that are usually racist. Keep this lens in mind when you are taking time to vet books on your shelves. This means we have to take the time to read the books we place on our shelves.

6. **Engaging and Relevant Stories:** We want to make sure that stories in the books have themes that are relevant for students such as family, love, friendship, death, school, etc. Also, take time to talk about these themes with students. When thinking of harder or more difficult issues in books, think about and talk about them from different perspectives. As a child, I wanted to see more than books about enslavement of Black folks, the genocide of Indigenous Peoples. I wanted to see books about folks like me living and going through what I am going through as a kid.

7. **Look at the Lifestyles:** Look for inaccuracy and inappropriateness in the depiction of cultures outside of dominant white society. Look at whether the characters/persons in the text and where they live, work, and go to school are depicted in a negative light according to what is the "norm" of the white majority. This could also be in the clothes they wear and customs.

8. **Weigh the Relationships Between People:** Look for how the relationships in the books are depicted. Ask yourself questions such as who may hold power? Who may be in a "supporting role?" How are the folks and the relationships shown?

9. **Check the Copyright Date:** The copyright date can be a very clear sign of whether a book is relevant and up-to-date in the growth of consciousness and evolution in society. It is different in various states; however, when thinking about nonfiction books on average depending on the topic, it should be no more than 5–10 years old. Fiction books can stay up-to-date longer; however, we must keep top of mind the eight steps prior to this one—especially relevance.

10. **Author/Illustrator Background:** This is important, especially when thinking about the content and who the content is about. The background of both the author and illustrator are important when thinking about books and illustrated in "own voices" (identifying as the same community of the book being

written) and whether they are qualified to write about the content of the book. Although there will and have been books written by folks who do not identify with the characters identified in the authored books, I believe it is especially important that the author has done their work to be able to write from a stance of the folks of that culture, race, or community.

Figure 4.1 shows each of the steps when vetting books for your classroom to provide more inclusive texts to infuse into your curriculum. This graphic is useful as a quick reference as you add or remove books from your library.

Taking time to vet the books on your shelves is essential; however, there may be some books that you may not have looked through with all of these factors in place.

Figure 4.1   Vetting books

There may be some books where you miss something—something that you overlooked. We are human. Remember when I learned about Dr. Seuss? It took a minute for me to do my own research on the history of Thomas Geisaleodore. When I found out the truth from my research and the research that was shared with me, I removed the books from my shelves—both at home and at school. It was simple. I did what I knew was right. Even though I had memories of reading the books as a child and reading those same books to my children, I made a choice for truth. I'm saying this to say that some books or authors you may find out later that they are not what needs to be on the shelves due to new learning and new growth—and that is okay. We listen, learn, do our own research, and make the changes that need to be made. As the great Maya Angelou said, when you know better, you do better. I am on a quest to do better and to continuously learn to know better. I hope you are, too. Part of that doing better is ensuring that the books on the shelves create mirrors for our students—especially our students from marginalized communities.

You Have Books with Mirrors! Now What?

Books alone without the internal and external bubble work cannot be transformative; however, reading books is a start. The work has to be done within you—the educator. What you believe does matter. Ultimately, kids can immediately tell if a teacher is inauthentic (children can read adults like a book!). So, we must believe in the power that books can have in education, in a child's learning, and in the work that we do each and every day. Do you believe that books can be healing? Do you believe that representation in books for children—especially those from marginalized communities—matters? Do you believe that, along with the books on the shelves, relationships are also vitally important in creating mirrors for our students? If you do, great. Then continue reading. If not, besides reading, there is more inner work that needs to be done and self-reflection to get to the root of the why behind the disbelief.

Once you begin getting the books, vetting them, and adding them to your classroom library, you must think about placing them on the shelves in inclusive ways. Do not just put the books in a bin entitled "Inclusive Books" or "Multicultural Books"—or put them out only if it is Black History Month or Asian American and Pacific Islander Heritage Month. No, no, no. Place the books on the shelves along with all the books. If you want to label a bin, label it "family" or "friendship" by the themes of the books. *Inclusive books* means just that—inclusive. That means even on your bookshelves.

Read to Your Students

I will probably say this in every single chapter, whether you teach students who are 5, 13, or 17: Students like to be read to, especially children's books. There is power in reading children's books to middle school students, high schoolers, and even college students. When you read aloud the book with your students, you have a shared experience with them. They have a shared experience with each other. This shared experience can breed really in-depth, impactful conversations about the book being read. This takes intentionality on your part as the educator.

First, make sure you have read the book prior for planning purposes. Next, take time to connect this book to the standards that you may have in your district. (Side note: Reading books and taking time to think critically about books is always part of the standards.) After you have done both of those things, create some questions that would elicit critical thinking and evoke conversation among your students. Having these questions ready to go at the beginning, middle, and end of the reading is essential. Sometimes, the conversation about the text goes even beyond your wildest reading conversation dreams and is so much richer than you ever could have planned for, especially when your students are used to reading inclusive books, talking about books, upholding community agreements, and respecting each other.

Healthy Dialogue and Discourse About Books (About Life)

When reading books, readers make connections. That is to be expected. Most often those connections are mirrors. When a student has a connection to a book and sees themselves in the mirror, it evokes passion and a sense of self-affirmation. That passion can manifest in many ways. Educators must realize this and expect it. This should also be known by the students. To have a healthy dialogue about books, the conditions must be set for this to happen. That means students have to know what is expected in the classroom community. Community agreements are a great way to have healthy discourse. Community agreements should be created by those in the community. That means time must be set aside for this to happen, and the agreements must be collaborated and agreed upon by everyone in the learning community. The following is an example of what the community agreements can look like with the focus on having healthy discourse.

Community Agreements for Discourse

These community agreements are a starting place when having healthy discourse surrounding books that are being read in the classroom:

- Take time to listen to what the person sharing is saying.
- Give everyone the space to share without interrupting.
- Have equity of voice.
- Respectful disagreements may happen, but it's important to share your reasoning.

Keep in mind that the passion that was discussed earlier shows up due to experiences that students have had or their families have had. This will also show up in different ways for students. The mirrors that they see can be self-affirming and can evoke a great deal of emotion. We are human, and because we are human, emotions will be present. Ensuring that we are setting the conditions for the discussion about books to be done in a healthy way is important. It is the responsibility of the educator to make sure this happens. Visit https://tinyurl .com/33nxpr6y to access "Sample Guidelines for Classroom Discussion Agreements," a great resource for helping create these environments from Brown University's Sheridan Center for Teaching and Learning.

This resource shares basic guidelines for sharing your thoughts, for responding to statements, and for listening and reflecting. Discourse is important. Feeling heard is important. It is also pertinent that we take time to create space for reading discussion and for the mirrors that are illuminated for students as well. The illumination is where the impact happens—it is where we begin to see the mirrors that the books are placing in front of us. It is also where we can look outside through the windows into each other's experiences.

Let's Reflect

1. As a child, did you see yourself in the pages of books that you read or that were read aloud to you in school? If yes, how did that feel to connect with the text that way? If no, how did that feel to not see yourself in the pages of books you read or that were read to you?

2. What does Dr. Rudine Sims Bishop's concept of mirrors mean to you personally? How can you intertwine your answer into the reading, teaching, and learning of the students you serve?

3. Have you taken time to vet the books on your shelves? If not, what actions will you begin to take to do so?

4. What comes up for you as you read this chapter? Take time to write.

Chapter 5

Learning: Opening Windows with Inclusive Text

Learn More

As I have taken time to reflect on my first window experience, the first time that I had a view of lives and stories that were different from my own, I know it was not in a school building. That may sound odd or shocking that my first memory of a window being opened to me wasn't in an official learning environment, but it wasn't.

I grew up in Woodbridge, Virginia, in the 1980s. Woodbridge is about 25 miles south of Washington, DC, and it was and is a melting pot of cultures and diverse communities. As I played outside in the yard or around the block, I made two best friends, Doris and Mani. Doris's family was from Greece. I remember going into her home with the smells of spanakopita being made, her Greek homework on her desk in her room (she went to Greek school on Saturdays), and her family speak Greek to each other. In our friendship, we would chat about her culture, the things they did, and about my own culture as well. We would talk about the differences and similarities of our cultures, and we both thought it was cool. We also wanted to learn more. It was amazing to learn about what made us different and what made us similar as well. I would try her family's food, which I loved, and she would try my family's food. We were best friends, and learning about one another was a gift to us both. That was a window that was opened to me at a young age.

Mani, who also lived down the street from me, was from India. Mani and his family would come out of the house at times wearing beautiful garments, long-buttoned shiny shirts, and sometimes headwraps. Later he would tell me about the special wedding he went to or another beautiful event. I remember thinking how beautiful they looked in the array of colors threaded through their silk-like clothing. I remember being curious about what it meant and knew it must have been special.

These memories of my childhood friends were some of my first windows. I am sure there are more, but these two shine the brightest at this time. They cultivated in me a sense of wonder—a wondering for my little self then and a wondering for myself now. Although Doris and Mani went to my school, I wonder what that would have looked like if I had been introduced and immersed in the windows in a school building? What would it had looked like if my teachers made us feel safe enough to come to school authentically and share parts of ourselves? What would that have felt like? How could I have had even richer conversations with my friends about their culture within the school building had I known more and had more knowledge—been introduced through books to more stories? What would that have looked like for my bubble, in schools, to be opened a little wider?

Let's Visualize

Let's take time to purposefully visualize what cultivating consistent, authentic window experiences could look like in a classroom or even beyond your classrooms. You may be visualizing what you would like to see on the walls, the shelves, throughout the lessons, and as part of the curriculum. All those components matter and even more can be added to create windows experiences. Expand your thinking outside of the bubble. Close your eyes. When you think of entering the lives and experiences of others, what are the possibilities for that expansion to happen in the classroom?

For me, as I visualize a classroom with windows, I visualize a teacher teaching a lesson and facilitating a discussion around a text that provides windows for some students and mirrors for others. Why do I include mirrors and windows in the same lesson? This can happen in any lesson. In any lesson that you are teaching, your students should be able to see either themselves or others in the lesson. As this is happening, I visualize students engaging in small group discussions around the text and pulling in experiences of the mirrors or the windows that provide a connection. They are engaging in conversations that provoke learning and learning for all. I hear the teacher asking thought-provoking questions that allow for critical thinking and healthy discourse among students. I see students writing about the text and offering window or mirror examples within their writing. I visualize them sharing their writing with others and getting both affirming and possible adjustments in their writing. I am looking at a place of beautiful community and enlightening engagement. This is mostly because of the teacher's intentionality of lesson planning, choice in diverse text chosen, and implementation, students feeling safe enough to discuss and more, which we will discuss later in the book.

Why Are Windows Important?

As a reader, I love reading a book that provides windows for me. It helps me to see the world, not just through my lens but also through the lens of others who may show up differently from myself. For example, although I identify as a cisgender female, my experience with reading, *Julian Is a Mermaid*, written by Jessica Love, and *King and the Dragonflies* by Kacen Callender was such a small peek into the lives of what children in the LGTBQ+ community may face. Those books, and so many more, are gifts to me. Windows offer that gift to the reader. By being able to connect to others through a window lens, it also allows you to peek into their bubble without popping it, which is almost like an immersion of some sort. The lens of a window may begin to change your belief about a person or group of people. It may help to break down bias, assumptions, and/or even stereotypes that had been created. That is why windows are so important and so necessary, especially in books. As my class collectively read, *Esperanza Rising*, written by Pam Muñoz Ryan, we had many conversations about the injustices that the Latinx community faced in the book. We also connected the book to the human rights of Latinx folks in the present. Reading this book allowed not only for window experiences but also brought in mirror experiences. By having the windows experience, it helped to open minds and hearts in the classroom. When students and even adults see others in books, it can begin to break down barriers that once stood tall. This may not happen overnight; however, if we continue to look out the window into the lives of others using inclusive text, it allows for a way forward into being better and a way forward to increase the level of engagement in classrooms all over the world.

Looking Out the Window
Cultivates Engagement

Students want to know about other people. They want to know about people who have similarities and differences from (compared to) them. The curiosity of a child is a great wonder. As an adult, childlike curiosity is what I often want to remember and cultivate. I want to cultivate that curious wondering in myself.

Getting curious about others with the release of judgment, having an open mind, and a desire to authentically learn is a wonderful feeling. It reminds us that we are in the midst of a community of learners. Learning about each other is a way to see each other. It allows us to practice perspective-taking and put ourselves (even momentarily) in the "shoes" of others. The same is true for classrooms. The majority of students are interested in learning about each other. That means how others identify, their religion, their culture, their orientation, etc.

This doesn't happen in an "othering" type of way, however. It happens in an innocently curious way. Othering is learned behavior. Canadian Museum for Human Rights states that the process of othering can be divided into two steps:

1. Categorizing a group of people according to perceived differences, such as ethnicity, skin color, religion, gender, or sexual orientation.
2. Identifying that group as inferior and using an "us versus them" mentality to alienate the group.

Before othering is learned, children have a true curiosity and wonder that comes from a place of innocence, not from a place of us versus them. They want the windows to be opened for them. They want to learn about people, experiences, and cultures that may be different from them. Books can initiate that window for students, and it can expand their bubbles and help them to tap into empathy, compassion, joy, and even celebration for the differences seen through the window. Reading books that create windows can help students to learn more about others. Reading books can begin to break down barriers and prejudices. The curiosity and wonder that children of all ages have for windows helps to initiate that process. Engagement is a large factor here. The wonder and curiosity that is already there helps to increase the engagement. It allows for space to absorb the reading, allowing the brain to take in the text and increasing the level of critical thinking almost simultaneously. This all can happen when the environment includes safety, acceptance, inclusion, and belonging. When the environment feels safe, the students are able to engage with each other, share their stories, read a variety of diverse books written by diverse authors, and discuss books openly. But how can you create that type of environment?

Cultivating Active Readers Through Windows

Cultivating active readers through windows means providing students with texts that allow them to see into bubbles that are different from their own—new worlds, perspectives, and even new views. This means exposing the readers to a variety of diverse and inclusive texts so students can see outside their bubbles. This encourages empathy, compassion, understanding, and connection. Cultivating active readers means teaching students to look at what they are reading critically. This helps them to analyze text in a critical way—thinking about themes, analyzing characters and author's intent in ways that allow them to have an open mind as well as a critical mind. When cultivating active readers through windows, it is also important for the teacher to model and scaffold reading skills to support and guide students to become more active, rather than passive in their window reading.

Creating an Environment of Windows That Cultivates Compassion

For students to feel comfortable to read, learn, and discuss outside of their bubbles, there must be an environment where the student feels safe enough to do so.

Teachers Doing the Inner Work

First, the teacher must have done their work to create such an environment. The inner work of a teacher in creating an environment where books are windows is important. For the teacher to facilitate lessons and discussions about mirrors in books, the teacher must also be reading and learning with text that includes windows for the teacher. When we ask students to do something, it is that much more impactful for the teacher to have engaged in it as well. So yes, the teacher must also be reading, learning, and growing where they are also immersed and connected to books with windows. I know teachers don't have enough time on their plates to read books, especially books outside of what they may be teaching. This inner work is not work that happens in one month or one year. This inner work and learning are ongoing. It is a learning that takes place over time. As a *poly reader*, a reader who reads many books at a time, I would say that you can read outside your bubble without finishing a book. You could read a chapter, an article, a podcast, or an audiobook. All of these forms of multimedia can help us to read and learn outside our bubbles and allow the windows to be opened up to us as educators. This is important because when we are immersed in reading outside our bubbles into the windows experience, we are able to teach and facilitate reading lessons more succinctly, with an open heart and an open mind, and it is ultimately more impactful. Your students see you as a reader and a reader of diverse texts. Students often emulate what they see. If they see or hear about you reading diverse texts, reading outside your bubble, they will be more inclined to do that too.

But most importantly, the reading and learning from the books read should expand outside of the diverse text you immerse yourself in. Teachers who are doing this work and the expansion of this work are also being the example in building relationships with their students, displaying authentic empathy, compassion, and care in ongoing ways. Teachers are building relationships that expand beyond just the surface level. Gess LeBlanc, author of *Who's in My Classroom?*, says that developmentally and culturally responsive teachers model empathy and care and make connections with students by purposefully seeking to learn about them, their families, and how they've navigated life both inside and outside of school. Reading outside of your bubble and allowing the windows to open is a necessary first step, an ongoing step; however, without the connection and care of humans and actions behind expansion of the bubble, it will not truly expand your world. It would just expand your bookshelf. We need to move beyond that. A teacher must be consistently building relationships with students, as well as learning about who they are through conversation, various experiences in the learning environment, learning, and reading. "Give students the opportunity to tell their story, to talk about themselves and their families, enables us to learn so much about them" (Creekmore & Creekmore, 2024). Reading outside of your bubble to expand your world is not the cure-all to creating a just world, but it is a way to model for your students, to create connections, and maintain relationships with students in the process. It isn't a one and done, it's ongoing. That is what lasts.

Creating Safety in the Learning Environment

Students enter the space and begin making a judgment call about whether the learning environment is one where windows are both accepted and celebrated. They make a judgment call on whether the learning environment is a safe place to be. One might say that when they enter that they get a "feeling" about the environment. Believe it or not, this happens even before the books open. This "feeling" may rise in their bodies upon entering the classroom. The student enters the classroom and takes time looking at the walls. They observe who is represented in the posters, they observe the types of books showcased on the shelves, and they observe how the teacher communicates with students as they enter the classroom. Does the teacher respond to some students one way and other students another way? Does the teacher smile as they enter?

These are all things that get vetted by students on whether the learning environment is one of belonging and inclusivity. So how do you as the teacher create an environment where students can feel the window environment before even getting to the books on the shelves? How do you create a psychologically safe environment? That is what we should **want**, and this is what we need. Science tells us that. In Zaretta Hammond's book *Culturally Responsive Teaching and The Brain*, she says that the brain needs to be part of a caring social community to maximize its sense of well-being (Hammond, 2015). She goes on to say that students of marginalized communities need to feel affirmed, nurtured, and included as valued members of the learning community.

We should **want/need** students to feel safe as soon as they step foot into our classrooms, and we **want** students to feel that they belong. Yes, we **want** the books on the shelves to do that too, and how can we create a space for safety and belonging in order for students to engage in the window books?

I would say this: Take time to build relationships with your students, and get to know them and their families beyond the surface level. The surface level is the niceties that happen during the school day. You probably already greet them at the door, check in on a student who may be misbehaving, and maybe even talk about a student at the family–teacher conference. But going beyond this surface level, take the time to have one-on-one conference times with students. It could be a "beginning of the year/getting to know you" conference, or it also could be a reading conference. These one-on-one times with just the teacher and the student can create connection. Learn about the student as a reader, find out if they like to read, ask what type of books they like to read, and offer books with mirrors and/or windows to the student. This allows the student to know that you see them.

Students can get lost in the learning environment. This can happen so easily, especially if the student is quiet, makes decent grades, and does what they need to do. I often call these students "ghosts in the classroom." I know it may sound a little harsh to say that, but I can honestly say in my years in elementary school, I was a ghost up until fifth grade. I didn't feel seen or heard by my teachers. Well, my fourth-grade teacher "saw" me, the ghost, when my grades started to slip, and she thought I was slacking off—turned out I needed glasses. That was the most attention she paid to me all year.

As an educator, I have always made it my business to not have students in my classroom that just float by, without me knowing or seeing them. All students should be seen in the classroom, and so should their families. They should never be ghosts. Even if you have multiple ELA classrooms on a high school block schedule, there should be time and space for relationship building. This is essential to the learning process. Without relationships, learning rarely takes place.

Create a Safe Space for Students

Create safe spaces, especially for students who identify as Black, Indigenous, and children of color, for them to feel comfortable sharing and engaging with diverse and inclusive texts. In the previous chapter, I noted ways to create an environment that exudes safety so that students are able to engage in reading and learning discussions around diverse texts. This includes the educator taking time to facilitate and create classroom agreements that surround these discussions. I have already provided some ways to do this in the previous chapter, but I wanted to reiterate that when talking about books that have windows, the conversations that happen, or the discourse that may take place are outside of our own stories or mirrors. When we are learning and reading about windows, there are many factors that come into play. The most important thing is to ensure that harm isn't done to students who are sharing their stories and lived experiences. We must make sure that as educators that we are observant and keenly aware of the level of vulnerability at play amid these "windows" discussions. We must foster a safe and open environment rooted in love, communication, honesty, and protection so all students feel embraced and held, especially students of color. We want our students to feel safe enough to contribute to conversations about diverse and inclusive books—books that they see themselves in (mirror books) and books that they see others in (window books).

Present Inclusive Instruction

Reading outside your bubble helps with teaching curriculum and instruction in inclusive ways. Just offering one culture is limiting to who we are in society. We are more than a single perspective—we are more than a single story. When we offer one textbook, one perspective, it keeps everyone in their individual bubbles. The diverse population of our world is beautiful. As educators, we have the world looking at us in our classrooms, in our learning spaces. When we just offer a single narrative to our students, it screams to students that only that single narrative is important. It tells them that the one perspective of a text is the only truth. We as educators know better than that. We know that when we offer a variety of perspectives and modalities for learning that we are giving our students a gift. We are giving them the gift of the expansion of their bubbles. We are offering students the movement from mirrors to windows. We are giving them a plethora of experiences and connections to relate to. This means we must take time to not just write a lesson for students but to create and craft that lesson for students. The difference between writing a lesson and crafting and creating a lesson is the deep purpose behind it. When we take the time to really think past the standard that the district has instructed us to teach and think about the purpose of teaching and integrate different perspectives of stories that are missing from the standard, we enter into creation mode.

We enter into the crafting and creating mode of curiosity and holistic teaching. We begin to ask ourselves whose bubble—what windows are not being seen here? We don't just take the standard and run with it, but we take the time to ask questions, to think of purpose, and to thread in the vision for student learning. The vision should always include the expansion of the bubble. The vision should always include your students' feeling seen. The vision should always allow students to walk away with not just answers, but questions.

Let me give you an example, when I reached the social studies standard about colonialism, I read it repeatedly. It wasn't that I didn't believe in the history from the books that as a grade-level team we were going to be teaching, but I had so many questions. I became curious about the outcome of the social studies lessons we started crafting as a team. No matter the subject in school, you are reading. I am not just pushing you to read outside your bubble in one subject area. They are all integrated, and reading should be threaded throughout your entire school day.

So, we began crafting lessons, and I had to push the pause button. I paused the creation of our lesson to ask very pertinent questions about the lessons. These were questions that I had even as a little girl in third or fourth grade. During colonialism, where were the Indigenous folks? The Black folks? Where were my people? We talked about them prior, but now they aren't in the story. Are you beginning to see the harm in just a single story? Colonialism is not just about the white folks who came to this land for religious freedom. That is just one perspective of the story. What about the folks who had their land and their freedom taken as a result for the other culture's pursuit of their freedom? When I paused the meeting, these were the questions I asked amid our lesson creation. They were questions that helped us grow as a team.

Our bubbles were expanding even, amid our creation of our lessons for our students—and we hadn't even taught it yet. We began to look for materials that included more than one perspective, more than one story. We found the materials, and together we crafted our lessons for the unit on colonialism. Was it perfect? Not at all. But it was a beginning of the expansion of our bubbles. We began reading first, we learned together as a team, and throughout the teaching of the lessons, we adjusted and made it even tighter and better each time. This began with curiosity and courage. As the only Black person in my team at the time, I had to speak up, and I had to use my voice, which is part of the learning ladder. After using my voice, I had to be honest, and I felt pulled to give students an accurate representation of history. We all wanted to teach truth, and that means including a variety of perspectives in the lessons. As a team, we took action, and we taught the lessons on colonialism from multiple perspectives. The kids really enjoyed reading, learning, discussing, and building their critical thinking skills through the expansion of their bubbles. Did we create mirror moments or window moments through reading? I would say we created both throughout our lessons—that is what it is all about.

Have Inclusive Texts on Your Bookshelves

I cannot overstate the importance of including these inclusive texts on the bookshelves. If you don't have these available, this would be something that I would discuss with the administration and/or the people in your district who makes decisions about curriculum materials. Teachers and students must have access to inclusive texts. I discuss accessibility in a later chapter. However, making sure the books are on your shelves to access during planning and instruction of the curriculum is crucial. When I say instruction, I mean all instruction. Inclusive books should be included in every subject—reading, writing, science, social studies, math, music, art, and physical education. In every subject there are inclusive books available they should be infused in the learning.

So, begin etching in your mind these words, "There is an inclusive book for that." The second thing you need to consistently say to yourself is "I need to learn, think, read, and plan outside my bubble." And it is true, you do.

Let me give you an example. If you are learning about space in science, maybe even specifically Apollo astronauts in space, you should be talking about Katherine Johnson, who was extremely instrumental in the return of the Apollo astronauts from the moon back to Earth. When learning about geometry, include in your lessons that Katherine Johnson also studied how to use geometry for space travel. When you are learning about social studies/history, you could also discuss how Katherine Johnson was the first Black woman computer scientist to have her name on a technical paper issued by NASA's Langley Research Center. You could also discuss the racism that she faced in being the first and only at that time.

So you should be saying, "There is an inclusive book for that, and that, and that." You should also be saying, "I need to learn, think, read, and plan outside my bubble." Then do just that—take action and teach your students. Expand your bubble. Take time to include those inclusive texts into your lessons. Just in that one example, you can see many connections to reading, science, and math. Not only does this provide students with learning into the windows of others, but it makes their learning relevant as well. Think about the amount of engagement that increases when students see their learning as relevant to their lives and the lives of others. Think about the questions you could ask throughout many lessons and the discussions that could take place. I just see learning overflowing—the learning of the students and the learning for you as a teacher. By providing the inclusive bubble-expansion texts that have windows, you are giving the students a gift of an open mind and open heart into the world, lives, and experiences of others.

Open Your Class to the Community

Bubbles are beautiful when they expand and even more beautiful when we can expand them into our communities. It is important to read and to connect to the windows we see in books. It is important to read and discuss the windows we read and learn about. However, when you see those windows live, it is powerful. This means bringing the community into the classroom to connect to the inclusive books you are reading about. For instance, if your students are reading and learning about the very first Black public librarian in Georgia, Annie L. McPheeters, then bring in a Black public or school librarian to your class. Have them come speak to your classes about what that means to them in connection to Annie L. McPheeters.

This is another great opportunity to teach a different type of writing, which is preparing for an interview, which is a research-based type of writing. My hope is by providing examples, this ignites your brain to get more creative and intentional in your teaching when thinking about reading and teaching outside your bubble.

Expanding outside your bubble starts and continues with reading, but it is much deeper than that. It is the action that is taken while that is happening. It is the reflective learning that is happening both individually and in community. The community that you have taken time to build and maintain in the classroom is the community that is also open to expansion. That expansion helps us to move from the windows in books to the windows in our daily lives. This is where pages come to life every day, offering a tangible experience applicable to our lives. We want those windows to influence how we show up, how we listen, how we respond, and how we learn from others. Windows within inclusive texts, once we turn reading and learning into action, is how books can transform our communities—and eventually our world.

Let's Reflect

1. As a child, did you see others that identified differently from you in the pages of books that you read or that were read aloud to you in school? If yes, how did it feel to learn about others through the pages of books? If no, how did that feel to not have the opportunity to learn about others through the pages of books you read or that were read to you?

2. What does Dr. Rudine Sims Bishop's concept of windows mean to you? How can you intertwine your answer into the reading, teaching, and learning of the students you serve?

3. What are some ways to build or continue building psychological safety in your classroom?

4. What are some ways that mirrors can cultivate engagement in your own learning community?

5. What comes up for you as you read this chapter? Take time to write.

Chapter 6
Learning: Gliding through Sliding-Glass Doors with Inclusive Text

Learn Some More

Using a window to see outside of yourself by way of reading is an important step into reading outside your bubble. However, the next step into being immersed into the lives, culture, and lived experiences of others is to glide through the sliding-glass door. Sliding-glass doors lead you to go outside your bubble and step into the houses and lives of others while reading.

When you read, this is when you take time to close your eyes and, through all your senses, imagine what someone else's lived experiences might feel like, look like, and sound like. A sliding-glass door by definition is a seamless transition from one space to another—usually from inner to outer. When you think about learning and gliding through the sliding-glass door when reading outside your bubble, you are actually expanding your bubble by attempting to step out of your space into the space of someone else—seamlessly. Although we know that we cannot know someone's experience completely, it allows us to peek in, even if it's for a moment, at what the experience might be like. This provides the opportunity of immersion while reading. It provides the opportunity of taking on—through imaginative lenses—the lives of others through not only reading but thinking critically, learning by listening, learning by discussing, and being present.

By doing this, sliding-glass doors offer the greatest reading tier for those who make the choice to glide through. A sliding-glass door is bigger than a window, as you read and step and expand through the sliding-glass door, you can see even more. It allows one to truly engage in empathy for others and their experiences. It allows for the ultimate perspective-taking hat to be placed on as you read. This action of sliding-glass doors can place you on the step of the learning ladder to make change.

Let's Visualize

Take a moment to visualize a sliding-glass door for yourself and for others. What could a sliding-glass door look, sound, and feel like in reading and learning for you and your students? Sliding-glass doors take reading and learning into even more action and even more engagement. It allows for readers and learners to take on the experiences of the lives, histories, characters in books, and real-life experiences of people who lived in this world through perspective-taking. They can imagine the perspectives of people who look like them—and those who don't. They can imagine people whose experiences are similar and those whose experiences may be or may have been different. This level of sliding-glass door in reading is one that moves the reader from looking out the window and taking the step into the reading experience through learning. That learning is perspective-taking while reading.

When I was a fifth-grade teacher for the first time, I taught with inclusive texts that provided windows and mirrors. Most of my students had gotten good at making connections to their own lives (mirrors) and looking outside of themselves and learning about the lives of others (windows). However, I wanted my students to dig even deeper into books that they were reading, and I wanted them to truly be able to immerse themselves in books that they were reading. I was teaching point of view to my students, and we were also engaging in a class-class wide book study on the book *Wonder*. *Wonder* is a book about a boy named August Pullman who was born with a facial difference, which had prevented him from going into a mainstream school. In the fifth grade, August decided to go to a mainstream school. When I think of an example of entering into someone's life experience through a sliding-glass door, I think of me and my fifth-grade students gliding into the life of August and his classmates. Teaching point of view while expanding outside of all our bubbles was an experience that I had alongside my students where we were able to read, buddy chat, discuss whole group, and truly engage in empathy, compassion, belonging, and acceptance in each chapter we read.

We began to take on and discuss in groups what the different characters might have been feeling in different chapters and situations that came up in the book. We discussed how August, his family, and his classmates might have been feeling in different moments and situations that occurred within the book. For instance, when August was being taken on a tour of his new school, some of the kids who gave the tour were being unkind and mean because of the way he looked. As we discussed, while most of my students understood that being mean to August was wrong, others thought they were just being "kids." We had opposing views. However, we discussed, and we moved through them to understand each other's viewpoint. We also took time to connect the book with our own lived experiences, as well. We moved in and out of the sliding-glass doors, and sometimes, during our reading, the students would see themselves in the book and connect with one of the characters. One student discussed how when they first came to our school, they couldn't speak English. They felt different and did not have many friends initially because of the language barrier. Although their experience was different than the character, August in *Wonder*, they were able to see mirrors while reading. When you expand outside of your bubble, the mirror experience can happen. This can happen where you, as the reader, can begin to weave in and out the metaphorical connection and perspective-taking of mirrors, windows, and sliding-glass doors as you are reading and learning. Amid reading, you may have that mirror experience and other times a window experience. As readers we are learners and we are also connectors, empathizers, feelers, friends—as we move through each of these layers while reading.

As we came to the end of reading *Wonder*, with me reading alongside my students, it allowed my students to also see me as a reader, a learner, and a critical thinker. I was able to authentically model the lesson on points of view of the varying characters from the book for my students. It helped to make the reading come alive because collectively we engaged in the book. It happened seamlessly and authentically. We were in flow. When students see you, as a learner, a reflector, a thinker, as well as their teacher, they begin to open up during reading even more, share even more of themselves and their thinking, and empathize and think critically about text by way of sliding-glass doors.

Why Are Sliding-Glass Doors Important?

Sliding-glass doors allow readers to be able to glide into a story and become a part of the world that the author has created. It allows the reader to open their minds to the world in the book, whether that world is fictitious or not. The reader becomes a learner by engrossing themselves in the words of the book through their imagination and open-mindedness. Sliding-glass doors make the reader feel transported into the author's world. This is where the greatest level of connection and empathy can happen.

Sliding-glass doors are important because that is where actionable reading can soar. Actionable reading is when the text that you are reading changes you. It ignites something in you. It moves you. The action first happens within yourself as you read. Then the actionable reading moves outside of self. For instance, when thinking about the book *Wonder* that I read with my fifth-grade students, the more we connected with the book, had group discussions, wrote about the book, and participated in group chats about the character August and what he endured in feeling "different" from his peers, when situations happened in the real lives of my fifth graders they responded differently than they would have previously in the year. When someone would feel othered or different in our class, students would often act differently and respond differently because of the discussions that were had about August in *Wonder*. They would make sure that all the students in our class felt included.

They also began to speak up and use their voices for each other in our classroom community. They would share at our classroom community meetings, and we would discuss as a group how we could show up better for one another in our learning community. There was a change that happened within my fifth-grade students as a result of the sliding-glass door moments that took place when reading the book, *Wonder*. Our students noticed it, and I did too. That change continued throughout the year. We often spoke about the connections we made to the inclusive books we continued to read during our community meetings. We talked about how we treat others that are different from ourselves even when we may not understand. We discussed what to do when we didn't understand, and we discussed what not to do. This is what sliding-glass door moments can do— they help us to remember our learning ladders. It helps to move into speaking out and making change.

Gliding through the sliding-glass door creates that change. They are just that powerful. There is power in books and how we engage in books. Initially, you may not notice the change within yourself or the change within others, but it is in the small moments of action that change can happen. It is those small ripples that can make a wave occur. Although one may think, oh, we are just discussing August in *Wonder*, that discussion can transfer to real-life choices in ourselves and in our students. It can transfer into our everyday lives and make us better— better readers, better learners, and better humans.

Gliding through Sliding-Glass Doors Cultivates Engagement

By the time a reader glides through the sliding-glass door, they are most likely already engaged in the reading. Whether the reader is an adult or a child, once they move through the sliding-glass door, they have already been engaged through mirrors and/or windows that they have connected with as part of their reading process.

However, the sliding-glass door offers another level of engagement. This level of engagement allows for light to enter, and the mind to be illuminated—just as the sunlight streams through the sliding-glass door. The illumination engages the reader with new ideas, new perspectives, and new knowledge to help the reader open their minds and hearts to another or a clearer understanding of the world. This level of engagement allows the reader to become part of the text they are reading. This is where the reader/learner is truly enmeshed in the text, in the story, and in the lives of the characters. Has this ever happened to you? It has happened to me. It happens when I am really getting involved in the book I am reading. I am so involved that I cannot put it down. I can imagine myself in the moments, in the lives, even as a character in the story, and my engagement has hit the roof. I am all in.

I have glided through the sliding-glass door into deeper imagination. Sometimes, as I read, I begin to think a little differently from that I had previously. It could be a belief that I had that I had been questioning or a situation that I initially thought differently about and changed my thinking. Oftentimes our thinking and our experiences have such a narrow view of what the world is or is not. Entering sliding-glass doors does expand our views of the world. It allows us to think differently as we engage in the pages of text. This is why we want our students to be as they engage in every book that they read. Just as I discussed about the book *Wonder*, the reader can begin to see a change in yourself and in others once you have entered the worlds of others that are outside of your bubbles.

The cultivation of engagement begins with knowing who your students are, what you need to teach, and choosing inclusive texts intentionally so that sliding-glass door moments are more likely to happen. As an educator, you can create spaces for these moments to happen. That means you as the teacher should/must also have the excitement and engagement of the books on your shelves. That encouragement from you must be authentic. We know that students see through inauthenticity. It needs to be real. We truly want our learning and excitement to be passed onto our students in authentic ways. We want our students to take the plunge into books that can be mirrors, windows, and sliding-glass doors for them as the reader, and we want it to increase engagement for them as well. That engagement will initiate curiosity, which can prompt the asking of questions to dive deeper into the text and get even more insight into the world they are entering through reading. You can create the moments for increased engagement and for sliding-glass doors to occur. The following are some ways to increase engagement:

Providing Choice

Allow your students to read books they want to read that are from different genres and reading levels. When readers can have agency to choose their books, the likelihood of engagement increases. I know as a teacher that there is some text that you will assign; however, when you can give opportunities for choice, do it.

Read-Alouds

Reading aloud to students can increase engagement in all readers at all levels. It can help to improve comprehension, vocabulary, and fluency. It can also create a relational experience between the reader and the students. Read-alouds can happen in any classroom at any grade level. It is a great way to get students interested in inclusive books that they may not have been interested in prior to the read-aloud.

Modeling Reading for Students

Even though we prepare the path for engagement, students must glide through the moments of engagement on their own. You as the teacher can make the path to reading actively so enticing that there is no doubt that the student would walk it.

Another powerful way to do that is by modeling reading for students. As the teacher, you can aid them in gliding into sliding-glass doors through modeling your thinking, modeling the use of your imagination, modeling your questioning, modeling your writing about the text, and modeling your reflection. Of course, all this should not happen in one sitting—that would be brain overload. However, this helps students to see the reading path that you, their teacher, take when expanding your own bubble. In almost every lesson that you introduce to students, you must be the model. You must show them your reading, your thinking, and your learning. Even if you are modeling in a content area that isn't reading, it is still important for students to see you model what reading looks like in various subjects. Taking time to model is important in increasing reading engagement through the use of sliding-glass door moments. As you take time to model for students, initially, the input may not match the output. It is important to note that every reader's glide into their reading engagement may look different and may sound different. Their paths, visualization, and understanding may also look and sound different. Readers are different, which is okay because everyone's engagement is unique to them. It is important for you as the teacher to share that with students as they are reading and understanding inclusive texts. We are human and unique in all our genius and learning. That is what makes expanding outside our own bubbles so incredible. We know that by planting the seed it eventually will sprout.

Cultivating Active Readers through Sliding-Glass Doors

It is also important to be the facilitator of your student's reading journeys. Part of that journey is moving into more active reading by passing through sliding-glass doors as they read text. Introduce diverse books to your class to create interest. Encourage your students to read books that have mirrors, windows, and sliding-glass doors threaded within them. We want the books they read to open your students to new perspectives and dig deeper than the surface level of the text. We want to cultivate active readers and can do this by guiding and facilitating our students to engage with the text in ways that strengthen their understanding and their critical thinking skills. We want them to read actively by digging deeper into the themes of the text and learn how to deeply analyze the characters as they read. Encouraging our students to think critically about the text through in-depth questioning and rigorous discussions is also important as they move from reading passively to being more active. We want students to take moments to connect with the text and reflect on what they have read. They can do this through discussions or written expressions. We also want to hear their voices of reflections and illuminations through their reading. For readers to do this in active ways, we must provide the support, facilitation, and guidance for students to navigate reading inclusive texts. Some of the ways that were discussed in which students can read actively are listed in Table 6.1.

It is important that students know we are there alongside them to provide a level of security as they read and learn outside their bubbles. Active reading has various strategies that allow students to take their reading from reading the words passively to being able to read, think, and discuss outside their bubbles.

Table 6.1   Reading Outside Your Bubbles: Increasing Active Readers through Sliding-Glass Doors

Annotation	Students can annotate the text as they read. They can write their thoughts, questions, and connections as they read the text. I suggest students annotate directly in the text they are reading.
Discussion	Students can participate in book chats, partner discussions, and book clubs to dig deeper into the text they are reading.
Research	Students can take time to research the content they are reading about to create a greater understanding of the text.
Compare and Contrast to Other Text	Students can compare and contrast various diverse texts and analyze characters, topics, or themes in the texts.
Connect the Text with Multimedia	Students can learn from other resources to relate the text to such as podcasts, articles, TV shows, and interviews.
Write about the Text	Students can write about the diverse text through reflection, reviews, or response to questions about the text.

Creating an Environment That Promotes Sliding-Glass Doors When Reading

As I have discussed in previous chapters, the reading environment that you help create with your students is so important. The reading environment should allow space for curiosity, exploration, and wonder. There are many pathways to create this type of environment, and I have covered some of these pathways already; however, here are some other ideas and pathways to take when creating a reading environment that is inclusive and helps to ignite reading.

Make Creative and Inclusive Spaces for Reading

Continue to create inviting spaces for reading. Make sure that the books you put in these spaces are inviting and create avenues for sliding glass doors moments to occur. This means you must get to know your students while also actively listen when they share about themselves and their experiences in the learning environment. By knowing your students well and listening to their experiences, you can intentionally add books that may offer a sliding door moment for other students. Make sure you display these sliding door moment/inclusive texts on top of bookshelves so that students can access them. We can also share one-on-one with our students books that may offer those moments for them. When we can make reading environments inclusive, open, connected, authentic, and inviting, it can help to promote engagement and active reading through diverse literature.

Continue to Share Inclusive and Diverse Texts

Make sure that you have available to students a wide range of text that allows not only students to see themselves and others within them. When you intentionally provide diverse text not only on the shelves but within your lessons, it allows for your students to explore, learn, and discover reading outside their bubbles. It is vital to take time to share and celebrate these books that are on the shelves in your classroom. Share snippets from inclusive texts that show students how the book emulates the reality of our world by having characters from a variety of cultures, backgrounds, orientations, and experiences. You can share these books in your community meetings, share them at the beginning of each week, or even have an author's study of the books in your learning community. Author's studies allow you to read multiple books by the same author and learn characteristics about the way the author writes, how they develop characters, and also see differences in the author's writing style.

Celebrate Diversity, Belonging, and Inclusivity

Take the time to intentionally celebrate the diversity within text and those who may or may not be a part of your community. Celebrate the diverse voices, cultures, backgrounds, and perspectives to cultivate belonging and inclusivity in your learning community. For example, we can take part in national awareness months, for instance, Caribbean Heritage Month, Black History Month, Asian American and Pacific Islander Heritage Month, Pride Month, etc. These celebrations allow students to see the importance of mirrors, windows, and sliding-glass doors.

This celebration of diversity should be happening in classrooms as well as the entire learning community. By celebrating and creating a culture of belonging and inclusivity, it increases the building of cultural competence but also increases awareness of social issues, historical events, and systemic inequalities. While celebrating is important, it is also important that we shouldn't celebrate only during the "appropriate" month; we need to schedule celebrations throughout the year. Empower students to become advocates and help create change in their communities. Celebrations help to bring joy and allow our students to feel seen.

Model Exploration

Use diverse and inclusive texts as displays in your room as well as read-alouds throughout a student's learning day. This allows for you to model the exploration that you want students to engage in as they are choosing to read books. We want our students to read different genres, authors, perspectives, and a variety of topics. This allows students to be explorers in their reading.

Model Being a Reader Yourself

Show students that you are also a reader of a variety of text inside and outside of your bubble. Allow them to see your excitement for books and your level of engagement with the books you are reading. When students see you as a reader, it opens a door for them as readers as well. By being a reading model, you are sharing with your students your curiosity, your experiences, and your reflection in your own personal reading journey. Creating a display of the inclusive texts that you are also reading can also help to ignite the flame in other students' reading journey as well as showing students that you too are a reader.

Allow for Discussion and Discourse

Once you have collaborated with students to create norms to have discussion and discourse respectfully, allow for that to occur. Let students read texts on varying topics. For instance, allow them to read about and discuss book bans. Create space for them to discuss their thoughts, their learnings, and their takeaways from the texts about book bans with one another. This discourse will have different views, and it may get passionate at times. However, facilitated discourse grounded in care, active listening and open hearts can help to cultivate perspective-taking. It provides practice for students to learn how to discuss texts and topics in open-minded ways.

Provide Reading Chats

Reading chats allow for you to get curious about the level of student engagement in your student's reading. It allows for you to ask questions that will allow you to see how much a student comprehends the book and to discuss with them any mirrors, windows, or sliding-glass doors within the text they are reading. These reading chats also allow for connection between you and the student. You can get to know them better, and they can also get to know you as well.

Let Students Share

Provide times for sharing in your reading environment. This sharing time can include times when students share about an amazing book they read that they feel their peers would really enjoy. This sharing time could be a time when a student may share a sliding-glass door moment for them. Sharing time helps to create a community of readers who feel safe enough to share their reading and learning with one another. It empowers the students in your classroom to use their voices and to believe that their voices matter. Remember to think about cultivating a safe environment for sharing. I spoke about cultivating a psychologically safe environment in the previous chapter. Psychological safety is pertinent for students to want to share and feel safe enough to do so.

Observe Your Reading Environment

Observe the rhythm and flow of your reading environment. Take time to look around, listen around, walk around, and take in spaces and parts of the day that your environment fosters reading outside your bubble environment. Take it in, take notes, reflect. Does my reading environment provide mirrors for all my students? Does it celebrate all students? Does it include all students? Slow down and observe. If some of these answers are no, make the necessary changes. You can even include your students in a reflection to get their input on their reading environment. By including them, they feel even more a part of the reading/learning community.

Readers Often Forget about Sliding-Glass Doors

The importance of sliding-glass doors when reading outside of your bubble is often a type of engagement that gets overlooked. This missing piece in engagement is probably due to not understanding what sliding-glass doors means and what it can look like while reading. It is my hope that, after reading this chapter, you will be able to grasp what it means to glide through sliding-glass doors while reading.

However, we don't want to miss this type of engagement when reading. When readers overlook sliding glass doors moments, going even deeper beyond the surface level into imagination and perspective-taking, it is often when the reader is struggling with comprehension and connecting with the text. Simply relying on the words and content of the text misses the essence of true immersion; as a result, you will lack seeing yourself in a mirror, others through a window, or even being able to enter through sliding-glass doors.

The lack of connection in a text can happen when the reader has not found alignment in their reading or may not understand the text enough to make a connection in a way that would immerse them by way of sliding-glass doors. This could be due to the difficulty of the text, fluency, or a lack of cultural awareness and/or situational awareness as students move through inclusive texts. This is why I stated earlier that reading chats and observations are so critical when getting to know a student as a reader. They can help with connecting and learning about themes and topics in the diverse books that they are reading. Having a reading chat will allow you to notice any confusion or misconceptions when a student is reading outside of their bubbles. It gives you time and space to help students enter through the sliding-glass doors through your facilitation, modeling, and scaffolding. Knowing this is also being keenly aware of the variety of reading styles in your learning community. I talked about knowing your students as readers in a previous chapter. While some students can enter through the abstract concept of sliding-glass doors on their own, other students may approach this level of reading through different paths. That is why it is essential to allow students to be immersed in reading alongside you, even if they are not ready yet to dive deeper into inclusive texts on their own. That immersion with you as a support will help to guide them into thinking deeper about diverse literature. It allows your students to continue to learn and grow at varying levels.

The concept of sliding-glass doors can offer readers impactful insight when reading outside of their bubbles. It can help your students to use the concept of visualization and imagination as they read, which can aid in opening minds and hearts to new ideas, cultures, perspectives, and worlds through diverse texts. This sliding-glass door metaphor, along with mirrors and windows, illuminates the transformative power of reading outside your bubble. It allows for the readers to become adventurers and explorers in their reading paths. It helps them to continue learning empathy, belonging, and acceptance through inclusive texts. Reading and reading actively allow for sliding-glass doors to emerge. This immersion and transformative power of inclusive texts can be transferred into the day-to-day lives of ourselves and the lives of our students. These concepts of mirrors, windows, and sliding-glass doors can help to make us better readers and better learners.

Let's Reflect

1. Have you engaged in a sliding-glass door moment as you read a book? What did that look and feel like? Take time to reflect on what it took to engage in the text to see the text through sliding-glass doors.

2. When thinking about cultivating active readers in your classroom, which of the strategies in Table 6.1 do you think would be helpful for your classroom?

3. What thoughts/ideas come up for you as you read this chapter? Take time to write.

Chapter 7
Equitable: Integrating Inclusive Texts in Equitable Ways

Equity

What do you think about when you hear the word **equity** as it relates to learning environments? Equity is an approach to ensuring equally high outcomes for all by removing the predictability of success or failure that currently correlates with any racial, social, economic, or cultural factor (Safir & Dugan, 2021). Educational equity is making sure that every student is taught at a high level, cared for with deep care, truly seen for their genius, and is given what they need free of biases each day. Equity is teaching and learning that is centered on justice, liberation, truth, and freedom, and it is free of bias and favoritism (Muhammad, 2023). You cannot have equity without the integration of reading and teaching with inclusive texts. If diverse books are not being threaded within the curriculum, then equity is not being attained in your learning environment. When you read, learn, and teach outside your bubble, what you get is the diverse experiences of what it means to be human in our world in a way that allows every child to be seen and feel a sense of belonging and acceptance. That is the essence of equity.

By ensuring that we as educators are equitable in integrating inclusive and diverse books within the learning—true, authentic, and holistic learning—we offer every child the foundation of what it means to be seen, heard, and valued in the world. That is the essence of equity. This work of equity is a journey and not a destination. This is ongoing work that we must do daily. Ensuring that we hold the lens of equity at the forefront of our work to see how we move in this world as humans will help us be able to focus on what is in fact inequitable in our classrooms, our schools, our school districts, and our systems. Let's put on our equity lens as we look at ways we can infuse inclusive texts in our curriculum for all students.

The Impact of Inclusive Texts and Equity

Equity and inclusive texts ensure that we hear stories from every single voice doing the storytelling. It ensures that we aren't just holding onto a single story and a single narrative. There can be danger in the single story because we are not opening our hearts and minds to the stories and perspectives of others, especially those from marginalized communities, the ones we need to read, hear, and listen to. However, hearing can be subjective. Sometimes we can hear, but we don't listen. Sometimes we hear, but we don't believe. When I say hear, I truly mean hearing in a way where we listen and learn from the storytellers. This is when we listen from our hearts—with equity at the center. It means taking the stories in. Whether we are taking stories in through reading, while actively listening, or sense making. We need to be able to listen with our hearts.

When we are taking the necessary steps to ensure that the integration of inclusive texts is equitable, it is essential that we dismantle the barriers that have pushed out the voices of the global majority, the voices who live at the margins. Those barriers can be societal barriers and sometimes the barriers can be within. The barriers are racism, bigotry, prejudice, biases, othering, and there are so many more. However, we must take the time to learn and unlearn, to release the barriers that can be standing in the way when putting equity at the forefront, when we are putting on our equity lenses. In the work of reading outside our bubbles, it means that we need to be putting these books of the unheard voices on our bookshelves, the authors who are being banned for their race, orientations, and/or the color of their skin. To continue to break down the barriers, we must choose to use those books, the books of the unheard to teach our students and expand their worlds. It means that we also not just have the books in our libraries, but we ensure that we integrate those voices into the curriculum. This allows their voices to be heard and for our students to learn from and feel seen in the process through the voices and the stories of others that have come before them.

Reading is the foundation of all subjects, and we need to include the stories that we haven't been including in our day-to-day teaching—not just in the midst of our reading segments. We want to include the stories that have been left out—ones that have been pushed out of the curriculum or was never there.

For example, when we think about teaching science, we may not think to include picture books to explain science concepts and inventions, or to allow students to see themselves in the field of science. Often, we are bogged down with so many standards to teach that we forget that this mirror/window creating connection piece is so essential. There are many great scientists who are unheard voices with stories that have been left out of the curriculum. Take for instance, the history of Native Peoples who have been inventors of some of the medicines we take today. There are at least 50 medicines today that have roots in traditional Native medicines used long ago. As teachers and students, we often only hear about Indigenous People in the content of social studies as it relates to history, not realizing how much of an impact Native People have made in science. Infusing this learning into the curriculum could look like in your study of rainforests and the destruction of rainforests, including the people of the rainforest. Reading a book entitled, *The Shaman's Apprentice: A Tale of the Amazon Rain Forest*, written by Mark J. Plotkin, which is a book about Tirio a Native boy who dreams of one day being the tribal shaman, and how he and his people learn the importance of their own knowledge about the healing properties of the rain forest. Infusing this book into your teachings and discussions about rainforest destruction can be powerful. Yet there are many Indigenous tribes in the Amazon rainforest, including the Yanomami, Kayapó, and Tikuna. In the Ituri Forest in northern Congo is home to the "Pygmies", including the Mbuti, Aka, Baka, and Twa. Then you have the Kombai tribe who live in Indonesia. All these different tribes in various parts of the world have contributed to the medicines we have today. Sharing this information with students allows them to have the mirror or window experience opening them up to learning they may have never had.

Cross-curricular connections can also have so much power, and students can absorb deep learning by exploring interdisciplinary connections. For example, Elbert Frank Cox was the first Black man to receive a PhD in math from Cornell University in 1925. Euphemia Haynes was the first Black woman to earn a PhD in math from the Catholic University of America in 1943. Those are just a few examples of excellence in math, and we could provide examples for any subject we teach students. The point is that we want to make it pertinent in our work to provide diverse examples and representation of folks from other races, cultures, and orientations. We want to do that no matter the subject that we teach or the grade level we have been assigned. This means having the lens of equity when we are planning, preparing, teaching, and reflecting is essential in integrating inclusive texts in equitable ways. It is taking into account that in whatever subject, standard, or skill we are teaching that we are teaching with our equity lenses on, and that lens is threaded in our work. Teaching with equity at the forefront of our minds takes reflection of teaching practices, acknowledgment and release of biases, ongoing learning, intention, and deep purpose to do this work well.

Whose Book Is Not Displayed?

As I have said repeatedly, to integrate inclusive texts in equitable ways, you must have a diverse collection of inclusive books on your shelves. Take the time to do this intentionally and to make sure you have the texts that you need. As you choose books, make sure you center the voices of those who have been historically underrepresented and those who have been unheard—voices of Black folks, Native folks, Latinx folks, folks of the LGBTQ+ community, and the Neurodiverse community to provide some examples.

In addition, you want to make sure that you are making it a priority that you have books authored by folks who have authentic voices and stories (what we may call "own voices") on your shelves. That means books written by folks from different races, backgrounds, genders, orientations, abilities, and socioeconomic statuses. These authors may be outside of your bubbles. However, prioritizing and amplifying the voices and perspectives of individuals from marginalized or underrepresented communities who have direct personal experience with the text is critical. This provides an authentic representation of the diverse experiences, identities, and cultures. Books with "own voices" as the authors allow for the depth and nuance that may have been missed in a book written by someone who doesn't identify with the characters or the experiences in the text being read. Own voices help the reader to cultivate more understanding of various cultures and/or communities written or illustrated by someone from that community. It helps the reader to build a greater appreciation for others different than them, their stories, and their perspectives. Books written by own voices can also disrupt problematic narratives and stereotypes that are often shaped by dominant perspectives. Supporting books written by authentic voices is looking through our equity lens because it also helps to address the inequities occurring in the area of publishing. By putting these books on the shelves, reading them, and teaching with books with authentic voices we are supporting the authors of the books. It allows the voices of the marginalized communities to be heard, read, and uplifted.

As I stated previously in the mirrors chapter, you want to have books that offer authentic representations of the books that you place on your shelves. Take the time to read, research, and sift through the books that you are putting in your book collection. It matters. You want to make sure that you are adding inclusive texts and teaching with these inclusive texts responsibly. Take time to review the steps I placed in the mirrors chapter to vet the books on your shelves so that you can integrate the texts in a way that is inclusive, fosters critical thinking, and promotes healthy dialogue amongst your students. By including diverse books, we want to create a sense of belonging, self-acceptance, acceptance of others, empowerment, and celebration as we look at and consistently add to our collection of books.

Integrate Inclusive Texts Equitably

Integrating texts within the lessons that you teach is something that some of you may do already. To integrate inclusive texts equitably in your curriculum and lessons, it takes not only selecting the books and aligning the books with the curriculum, but it also involves intentional planning. When you are lesson planning and you are dissecting the standards to teach, take time to think about which voices are not heard and which voices you could lift up simply by choosing the "just right" inclusive text for your lesson. The standards oftentimes don't include folks from marginalized communities, or they focus on the same diverse trailblazers year after year. Make sure that you read through the standards with a critical eye and include the voices that were missed.

Choosing books that align with your lessons can be found in many places. However, there are a few staple websites that I go to find them: We Need Diverse Books, Social Justice Books, Disrupt Texts, Read Across America, and Colorín Colorado. Just to name a few. Here is an example of infusing inclusive text equitably. Although you may be teaching a skill around alliteration or repetition in poetry, take time to choose a book that highlights that skill in their poetic flow written by an author from marginalized communities.

Show the students a picture of that person/human, describe who they are, and share other books or poems they have written. This can sound like, "This poem that you just heard entitled, 'Bless This Land,' is written by Joy Harjo. She was the Poet Laureate of the United States. A poet laureate is a poet officially appointed by a government who creates poems for special events and occasions for the country. Joy Harjo is a member of the Mvskoke/Creek Nation. She is the author of many books of poetry, including *An American Sunrise*. This is a picture of Joy Harjo." Then continue to teach your lesson on alliteration to your students using Joy Harjo's poem. What this does in that brief but impactful introduction is it provides a mirror or window for your students in your classroom.

Just sharing about the author/poet, who they are, their picture, and their work can allow a child in your room to say to themselves, I, too, can be an author or poet. It also opens their world to the work of Joy Harjo and students may just continue reading other poems by Harjo.

I remember in tenth grade during my creative writing class, I was introduced to Langston Hughes's poem "Mother to Son." My teacher Mrs. Hailey used this poem to teach with, to have us discuss, and to emulate Hughes's style in our own poetry. Mrs. Hailey opened the door to my love of Langston Hughes. She allowed me to see a mirror in poetry. I began writing poems, and Langston Hughes is still one of my favorite poet. Just as I said earlier, windows and mirrors can happen in any subject throughout your school day and at any age in a student's learning journey. It often happens in the seemingly smallest of moments of teaching, reading, and sharing.

Promote Discussion

As you are teaching your lesson, either at the beginning, midway through, or at the end, it is imperative that you provide space for dialogue and discussions. This is encouraged to deepen their understanding of the text and to create spaces for your readers to offer varied perspectives during the discussions. This is also a great time to allow students to ask questions and for them to take time to learn from each other. This type of learning helps to promote critical thinking and critical reading skills. These types of facilitative discussions and dialogue allow us, the teachers/facilitators, to aid in navigating topics such as racism, sexism, and discrimination. It allows us to be able to have discussions such as these in a responsible way. Yet it provides space for students to discuss these important topics.

It is important that, as the teacher, you prepare for these topics of discussion. I would suggest preparing ahead of time. Try to imagine what types of questions students may ask or questions that you have thought about yourself. This will help you to navigate them more easefully. There may be times when you may feel uncomfortable and uneasy about having these discussions; however, the world we live in and the world our students live in calls for these discussions to be had. We have to push past our own discomfort to ensure that we are teaching our learners to read and think and learn outside their bubbles. And that means us—the teachers, too. Remember we are all learners and when we know better, we do better.

Doing better means that we take the time to not sweep issues under the rug but to bring them to the surface and allow our students to be thoughtful thinkers and rigorous reflectors. Integrating literature and having discussions about literature that sometimes brings up issues that our society faces today or has faced in the past is a way to transform the system that wants to hide true history or that wants to ban books. These discussions may be uncomfortable; however, we can all learn amongst the discomfort. Ask yourself where does the discomfort come from? What is the root of the discomfort? This feeling may feel different for some than others. Taking time to sit in that discomfort is a beginning. But you can do it. We can do it. We need to do it.

Modeling with Inclusive Texts

Another way to learn how to integrate inclusive texts as part of your teaching is by asking an instructional/literacy coach—or if you don't have one, a fellow peer who does this effectively—to model for you. Our teachers in the next classroom can often be the best professional learning partners. This also helps build collaboration and cultivate a learning community in schools.

As an instructional coach in schools, I would intentionally model lessons using inclusive texts. The hope in doing this was that in seeing me modeling with inclusive texts, then the teachers would also do the same. When teachers would invite me into their classrooms to model a variety of lessons in their classrooms, that is what I would do as I planned the lesson or co-planned the lesson with them. Once when a teacher asked me to come in and model the fairy-tale lesson to her students, I intentionally chose *Petite Rouge* by Mike Artell. *Petite Rouge* is the Cajun version of *Little Red Riding Hood*. This book was near and dear to my heart because I am of Creole descent. Although there are differences in being Cajun and Creole, there are some similarities as well. I was able to read the book with an accent from my Creole culture, as well as share with students things about my culture, for instance, what boudin is and the significance of the swamp gator, Claude. In the midst of my own mirror in this story, I was able to simultaneously provide mirrors and windows for the students in the class and for their teacher. During the lesson, students began discussing not only the essential parts of a fairy tale but the significance of varying aspects of cultures that have fairy tales. They began comparing and contrasting what they noticed from the two tales.

This opened their world to other cultures' fairy tales, and the students wanted to learn more. A couple of weeks later, as I was observing classrooms, I observed the same teacher that I had modeled Petite Rouge to sharing *Yeh Shen: A Cinderella Story from China*, by Ai-Ling Louie, with her students. I was very excited and hopeful to see that, and I shared that with the teacher. There is power in modeling and allowing teachers to see the integration of inclusive texts in action. It could start with you. Just as I started a ripple, it was important for another teacher to start a ripple with me. It is better in community.

Community and Equity

One thing about ensuring you are integrating inclusive texts equitably is to consciously be in community with other folks willing, acknowledging, and advocating the need for the work. Community and equity are interconnected. They both have impactful and significant roles to ensure that our learning communities are inclusive, foster belonging, and offer the gift of acceptance. This means that what we offer our students as we aid them in reading outside their bubbles in safe and welcoming environments, that we also offer that same safe space for the teachers that teach them.

Together, in community, we can advocate for a culturally relevant and inclusive curriculum that reflects the diversity of student backgrounds, identities, and their experiences. We need to do this equity work in community—together. We need each other, and we also as teachers need an equitable learning environment to teach from as well. We want to ensure that not only our students are thriving, safe, and feel seen and heard in the learning environments, but that we create that same safety, feeling of belonging, and acceptance for teachers to ensure that they can thrive. We are all interconnected. If we make sure that we have an equitable and inclusive community for all, we can continue to do that same ongoing work for our children. This helps all of us contribute to the collective well-being for us, for our students, and for our learning communities. Doing this work alone as an educator can be rewarding and impactful; however, doing this work in community with others can have a much greater impact. When we remember that collectively we can create equitable spaces where we include inclusive and diverse texts in our curriculum, we all win. Our students win, and we win as educators. When communities come together to prioritize the needs of all students, teach them at high levels, and expect that they will learn at high levels, we can create more inclusive and equitable learning environments where every student can showcase their geniuses and thrive.

Let's Reflect

1. What does equity mean to you? What does it look like in your learning community?

2. Equity lens is a term that is used in this chapter, has there been a time when you placed on your lenses and had to advocate for something that was inequitable? What happened? What was the outcome?

3. Think about your learning community as it relates to reading outside your bubble. Where could your learning community do better in this area to make it equitable for all students?

4. What comes up for you as you read this chapter? Take time to write.

Chapter 8

Access: Getting Inclusive Texts into Everyone's Hands

Access

Access to inclusive books is so critical in promoting representation, inclusivity, a sense of belonging, acceptance, and care. Making sure that all folks in the learning environment have access to inclusive texts is essential not only to the learning of students but to their well-being. There are many ways to get books into the hands of students and teachers. This should be a goal for all learning communities. At times, it can seem like a daunting task, but it can happen. As I said previously, it has to be a value and a priority that the community holds dear in the learning environment. Once you have set the goal of prioritizing inclusive texts in the learning community to ensure that lessons are culturally responsive and include inclusive and diverse literature, then accessibility isn't so daunting.

Being a classroom teacher who provided a culturally responsive education that included diverse literature to my students was my goal. I often would purchase books on my own, out of my pocket, because I didn't think my school had the funds as a school and wanted the books as my own. I wanted to build my classroom library. As I taught, I would take time to integrate inclusive, diverse books into the lessons. I would model with the books, integrate the books in all content areas, and conduct read-alouds and discussions, and I would ensure that the inclusive texts were accessible to students on my bookshelves.

But books can get expensive, especially when you are on a teacher's salary. Because of that, I began to use my voice through the use of my weekly teacher newsletters. I would send home the book pamphlets from Scholastic Books for students to be able to buy books for their home libraries, and I would get points.

It was a win-win because building a home library is so important for students to know that literacy is not only important at school but at home as well. Then I would use my points to get more books for my classroom, and it helped me to build a more diverse book collection for my students to read throughout the day. I wanted to make sure that students had what they needed to feel seen, heard, and valued.

Even as an instructional coach, I wanted to make it a goal to ensure that our school had access to inclusive books in classrooms for teachers and students to teach with and read. As a coach, I would investigate the classrooms and the school library for resources I saw that were needed in our school community. As I observed, I became keenly aware that we needed more inclusive and diverse books in our school. We had some in our library and in classrooms, but we needed more—so much more. We had students who needed to see representation in the books that they read. It was critical.

I decided to use the influence that I had as an instructional coach to utilize my voice and advocate for buying more inclusive books for teachers and students. I spoke with leadership, and we came up with a plan. I took time to dissect the state standards for each grade level. I chose to begin with science standards. I wanted to begin with an area that at the time had the greatest need. I began to research inclusive books that teachers could use with their students in their lessons as they taught the standards. I looked at First Book Marketplace. This was my go-to resource to get diverse books in the hands of the teachers and students in the building at a reasonable rate. I also was able to purchase books from Amazon in bulk at decent rates as well.

I began adding inclusive texts to our science resources because I noticed, at the time, that it was the content area that was lacking when thinking about books with diverse people and experiences. After meeting with my principal about the lack of representation of books in this subject area, we discussed a plan and included the purchase of these books in the school-wide plan and budget. A couple of months later, we had inclusive books for science standards for every grade level. It was exciting to open the boxes and be able to sort the books in bins for the grade-level teachers to use and share. Some of the books that we added were *Women in Science* by Rachel Ignotofsky, *Mae Among the Stars,* by Roda Ahmed, *Born Curious,* by Martha Freeman, *Hidden Figures* by Margot Lee Shetterly, *Whoosh! Lonnie Johnson's Super Soaking Stream of Inventions,* by Chris Barton, to name a few. Although it may have seemed like a small act, that is how you begin to make change. We needed to increase access to inclusive texts, and I used my influence and my voice to help make those changes. Even as a teacher in the classroom, I used the power within my four walls to make changes at the classroom level. As an instructional coach, I used the influence I had to use my voice to make inclusive and diverse texts accessible to all. It was a small step, but a mighty one to ensure equitable access for students to learn and for teachers to teach with.

Ways to Get Access to Inclusive Books

There are a few ways to ensure access to inclusive books in your learning communities and in your own classroom. I will walk you through a few paths that I have personally taken and that others in the field of education have taken as well. As you read through these various pathways, think about using these paths in creative ways in the learning environments where you teach.

The School Library

Get to know and set up time to talk to your school librarian or media specialist. In most cases, the school librarian has some funds to purchase books for your school. They sometimes have the agency and funding to put books on the shelves in your school library. Being that the library is and should be the hub of the school, the goal is to put as many books in the hands of students as possible. Those books should be books where the children can see representation of diverse people in the books. They should be books that have mirrors, windows, and sliding-glass doors in them. Not only will this increase engagement, but it will also increase accessibility.

Ask the librarian if you can give them some suggested titles that they want to add to the library. If you need help looking for titles of inclusive books, there are books posted on my Instagram page @loveteachbless and my website, Love. Teach. Bless, and others do this work like authors and book influencers Charnaie Gordon from Here Wee Read, Vera Ahiyya, The Tutu Teacher, and many others. Share those titles with your school and local librarian. Once the school librarian purchases these books and can track just how many of the diverse and inclusive books are being checked out by students, they will be able to see the increasing need for them more and more. They will place them in their budget. This also leads to having inclusive books at book fairs and author visits as well.

The librarian in the school where I worked began to connect with the local bookstores, too! When authors of books would come to the local bookstores to share their books, they would also come to our school. What this did was it allowed for kids to get excited about books! It allowed them to see authors of diverse backgrounds. It gave kids access and got our students interested in the author's books. For example, we had authors and illustrators visit like Derrick Barnes and Vanessa Brantley Newton who wrote *The King of Kindergarten*; Kwame Alexander (Figure 8.1) who wrote *The Crossover*; and Shelli Johannes who wrote *CeCe Loves Science*. Note: I do realize that in some states and school districts, the banning of books, especially books written and illustrated by authors of marginalized communities, is happening at alarming rates. I will talk more about this in Chapter 10.

The Public Library

Although it is nice to have your own collection of inclusive books, having access to the public library, especially as a teacher, can be an invaluable resource. So, get a library card and suggest that your students get one too. As a classroom teacher, I would go to the public library almost every week. The librarian knew me by name at one point.

Figure 8.1 Kwame Alexander on tour

I would look through the next couple of weeks of lesson plans and our state standards, and I would take my little wagon to the public library. I would get so many books that represented the world and also aligned with the standards. I would get books to teach with, and I would get books to display. My students would be engulfed in books that looked like them and others and it also increased engagement a. This was a great, free way to make books accessible to my students. Other teachers would borrow some of the books as well. That little ripple or wave moved into the classrooms of other teachers also allowed for other students to have access to the inclusive texts.

Writing Grants

Writing grants can feel like such a daunting task for most educators. Before I wrote a grant myself, I would shy away from grant writing. I would think that I had to have a certain writing or skill set to write a grant. I guess it was a bit of imposter syndrome or lack of hope that I would get the grant approved. Until I did it.

I wrote my first grant to get books into my classroom—inclusive books for my students. And guess what? It was not as challenging as I thought it would be. Did it take time to write? Definitely. But I took the time to write it. If there is money out there that can help me give my students access to books and what they need, why not do it? When writing the grant, I had to include the why—the reason for the need. I included some research about my school, the demographics of my students, and just wrote from my heart about the need for students to be represented in the books they read. I got the grant approved! I was able to put even more books on the shelves for my students to see themselves. I was able to model using inclusive text, as well as making books that represented the world that we live in more accessible for the students that I served. There are many places to find grants for teachers. Often your state will have grants for teachers that often districts have the information to share. Some other grants out there is the Bill Gates Foundation, International Literacy Association (ILA), Aldi, Dollar General Literacy Foundation, and DonorsChoose. Those are a few places to begin to write grants to receive books for your classroom and school to increase the accessibility of books for students.

Books Digitally

I love putting actual books with spines in the hands of children. I love them to touch and smell the books that they are reading. Yes, I do that. However, the truth of the matter is, in the digital age that we are in, students are reading online as well. I have my own thoughts on just how much time students are spending online, but this is the digital world we are in. There are inclusive and diverse books online that can also provide access to our students. It is another avenue for accessing diverse books. This is especially helpful when students are not able to go to public libraries or when they are at home and may not have a ton of books on their bookshelves to read. This investment allows for students to have access to e-books, audiobooks, and digital magazines as well. This gives students multiple pathways to reading and engaging in inclusive text. It expands access to inclusive texts even further, and it also allows students to keep up with the digital world. This is not just the wave of the future—this is our present. Digital access to inclusive texts is just as important when used responsibly and in a balanced way. One great way to provide access to digital text is through a free resource called EPIC. I absolutely love this reading resources because it is free for teachers, and it allows students to read digitally.

Allow the Texts to Be Seen

Do you remember going to the school library as a child looking at all the books displayed on the tops of shelves and choosing one of them to check out? I do. First of all, thanks to the Dewey Decimal System, where we were only able to find books in the book catalog if we already knew that the books were there. It's a cherished system by many that helps put our books in a systematic, yet not equitable or accessible, manner on the shelves.

Unless you knew the exact book or subject matter you wanted, it was not particularly helpful in knowing whether or not a book is going to be one that you will be engaged in or that you will connect with. Although we shouldn't choose a book by its cover or who is displayed on it—we do. This is called *book bias*.

Book bias is the tendency to favor certain types of books over others. It can be based on personal preference, cultural norms, or societal stereotypes. The bias can show up in several ways. A reader can hold a book bias toward the author, genre, content, representation, or language biases. To think about increasing accessibility to inclusive books, it is important to take the time to discuss what book bias is with students. Doing this helps to expand our reading bubbles and challenge our assumptions. When we expand our bubbles and release book biases, we will be more able to seek out diverse voices and perspectives. So, it is important that a variety of covers of books are visible to students and that we take the time to introduce students to a variety of books. That increases accessibility even more than the books just being on the bookshelves. Take the time to showcase books on your shelves, on the whiteboard stand, and on the tops of tables. When students see inclusive books being displayed, it says to them that the books are important—that they matter. It is a subtle yet bold way of showing students the importance of making sure they have access to books that they can see themselves in—that they can see their classmates in.

These different pathways are a few ways to begin in making inclusive text accessible to students and teachers in your learning communities. By taking a path to implementation in getting these books in the hands of students, you are ensuring equitable access to books that promote a sense of belonging, inclusivity, representation, and acceptance for all readers in your learning communities. Accessibility is one step to expanding the bubbles and reading outside of our bubbles.

Make Teaching and Learning with Inclusive Texts Accessible

Having diverse books on the bookshelves is a great start. We have already discussed many ways to integrate these texts into the curriculum throughout the "L" chapters. However, I am going to double down on a few more strategies to ensure that these inclusive texts are accessible to all.

You Value What You Budget

Making sure that funds are allocated for the purchase of inclusive texts for the learning community is essential. If books, especially inclusive texts written by own voices, are not a part of the budget, you should advocate for funding to make sure the purchase of inclusive texts is a priority. You value what you budget.

Integrate Inclusive Texts into the Curriculum

I will reiterate this point—take time to integrate inclusive texts into all subjects and in all grade levels. Include texts by authors who have own voices. Include these voices in your mini-lessons, class discussions, projects, etc. This increases accessibility of the texts. Sometimes access is decreased not because the text is not available, but because it hasn't been introduced, read, or taught to the students. We increase access when we take the step from having the books on the shelves to using them in our curriculum and our teaching.

Whole Class or Small Group Book Studies

Having book studies increases engagement and also provides accessibility to inclusive texts. Use diverse books for students to explore and discuss the texts within your supportive learning environment. Over the summer, my daughter and her friends created a book study using the book, *Grounded*, by Aisha Saeed, S. K. Ali, Jamilah Thompkins-Bigelow, and Huda Al-Marashi. My friend and I took them to the bookstore and showed them many diverse books to choose from. They had to make a unanimous decision on which text they were going to read. *Grounded* was the winner for my daughter and her two friends to have their summer book study. Although *Grounded* was the winner and they had a blast reading and discussing it during their ice cream dates, they were introduced to so many more diverse books to add to their reading lists. They were given access through invitation. As we moms were introducing different books to our kids, each time they received another book recommendation. The same thing can happen in your classrooms with your students. Introduce a variety of inclusive texts to your students and create small group book studies. I have even seen teachers do room transformations and change their classrooms to coffee shops to increase engagement. This gets kids excited and talking about books in a fun way.

Author Visits

Author visits are a great way to open the world of inclusive books to students by way of the actual author. Remember when I said earlier in this book that my son became attached to books written by Kwame Alexander? Well, he came to my school! He was doing pop-ups around the United States at various schools in his *Rebound* tour bus, and I messaged him to come to my school—and he did! The kids were so excited to see an author, a Black author, and an actual tour bus pull into the parking lot of our school. He was a superstar—the students were so excited and so was I!

Student Voices

Empower your students to use their own voices to advocate for inclusive texts in your learning communities. You can have students share the diverse books they're reading and recommend them to their classmates and other students as well. The morning announcements is also a great place to allow students to use their voice. When I was teaching fifth grade, I had a bulletin board of book recommendations. Students would recommend books they deemed as five-star books for their classmates to read. On these pieces of paper that they would post, they would color in how many stars the book received from one to five. They included a summary of the book and the book's title and author. In a few schools in which I worked, we had book recommendations on the morning announcements. The students would share their names, the book title, a summary of the book, how many stars they would give it, and why. Students would listen in and see if the book recommendations made them want to check out the book from the library. It was so interesting to see how much the book recommendations were being used by the students in the learning environment. It provided the students with the empowerment they needed to use their voices and share books.

These are just a few strategies that learning communities can use to ensure that students have access to inclusive and diverse books that show who they are, who others are, life experiences, and more. Accessibility to inclusive texts is important. Every learning environment should make this a priority in their budget. Access to books helps to ensure that the resources are available for students and teachers to use. It is equally important to take the next step in moving books from the bookshelves and into the hands of students. It is essential to take the time to provide professional learning to accompany the integration of inclusive texts in lessons. Teachers must learn strategies and skills to integrate diverse books in effective ways. Professional learning—the "P" is the last portion of the LEAP Framework. It is another essential component that learning communities need to be able to intentionally and purposefully integrate inclusive texts into the curriculum.

Let's Reflect

1. What are some ways in your learning community to increase access to inclusive texts to your students?

2. Which of these strategies listed in this chapter are ones that would help to make reading, teaching, and learning more accessible to students and teachers in your learning community?

3. What comes up for you as you read this chapter? Take time to write.

Chapter 9

Purposeful and Professional Learning: Building Skill and Routine to Transform Teaching and Learning

Purposeful and Professional Learning

Let's be honest, professional learning is an area that can be viewed as friend and/or foe. Oftentimes, educators are sitting in spaces where professional learning is just another check off their to-do list or a directive by leaders. Sometimes they do not see the need for the learning or how it can impact their teaching or the learning of their students. However, when the learning is purposeful, meaningful, relevant, and psychologically safe, it can be an area of growth and even excitement for educators. When providing professional learning for educators, especially in the area of integrating inclusive texts into the curriculum, it is important to take time to hone in on the purpose and relevance of the learning being offered.

As an instructional coach, I would provide professional learning focused on reading/reading strategies. I often noticed that some teachers who attended the sessions that weren't specifically reading teachers would be disengaged. I would often think that because they weren't the designated "reading teacher" they felt it wasn't relevant. Some teachers even said they didn't need to be included in the professional learning because they didn't teach reading.

But reading is entwined in all *subjects*. All teachers are reading teachers. When you integrate inclusive literature in a way that is threaded within varying content areas, you only magnify the teaching and learning taking place within each content area that is being taught to students. When all stories are shared and all voices are heard, the level of learning and engagement in the learning can only increase. When students are empowered with literacy-building skills across different content areas, as well as being able to expand outside of their bubbles, they can think even more critically, hold in-depth discussions, and build connections at home, as well as with peers and community members. Students develop their ability to perform as problem-solvers and good citizens when they can make sense of the information, find the information relevant, and break down facts and opinions by way of learning about diverse perspectives, communities, and cultures using inclusive books. The ability to process information, hold conversations, and formulate thoughts related to their prior learning allows students to excel in each content area (Vasquez, Sanchez, & Kozimor, 2021). That level of excellence is increased when students can read and learn inside their own bubbles and expand the worlds of others.

We want our students to excel in all content areas, so we provide them with a thread of literacy that is inclusive and diverse within the varying content areas they are taught, which contributes to their thriving. To do this, we must ensure that the teachers in the classrooms are equipped to provide the level of instruction not only where students are learning the skill of reading and comprehending text, but also seeing themselves and others in the text that they read. We must provide professional learning to all teachers in not just reading outside the bubbles for them and their students but teaching outside their bubbles, too. We want teachers teaching at high(er) levels and having that same level of expectation for our students. We want our students to learn at high levels. Teachers must ground in the purpose and move into this action. To do so, curriculum leaders in schools must provide professional learning to teachers to give students the teaching and learning they deserve.

Before Professional Learning

When thinking of professional learning, I am mostly directing this section to leaders of learning communities, whether you are a teacher leader, an instructional coach, an assistant principal, or a principal—anyone who is responsible for leading or making decisions about professional learning of teachers. Teachers, this chapter will benefit you also as you take ownership of your learning. You need to know what learning you should be engaging in and the type of professional learning that you should be advocating for. Professional learning is important to the growth of all educators. However, in thinking about the folks who are leading the charge, I want to make sure that the professional learning of the teachers in your building is a priority. Especially, professional learning around effective integration of inclusive texts in learning communities. Learning how to do this work is important and putting the *how* into action is just as important.

As the facilitator of professional learning or even if you are learning on your own, it is important to know there may be some hesitancy in providing professional learning in inclusive texts. One may be hesitant because they do not want another "thing" to integrate inclusive literature in their content areas. Whatever the hesitancy may be, we must also know and be cognizant that incorporating literacy that is inclusive and offers diverse perspectives within varying content areas increases student learning. When students are taught using curriculum and texts where they feel seen, heard, and valued and others do too, their learning skyrockets.

First Steps

When thinking about how to incorporate or begin professional learning, the facilitator of this learning must be knowledgeable about the purpose of professional learning—the *why*. You need to know the purpose to be grounded in it and for it to be your anchor in this work—for the teacher to also anchor in this work. The purpose is what is going to create buy-in from your teachers. You may think if you are someone who already believes in this work and may even be doing this work every day—it may be hard to even take in that you must create buy-in for educators to do this good, impactful work for students. If that is you, it just means that you already have seen and/or believe in the power of inclusive texts in student learning. However, with the nature of the climate we live in—we must facilitate the process of regrounding. We can lead the charge of regrounding. As facilitators, we need to ensure that every student sitting in those chairs feel seen, heard, and valued in the lessons they are learning. Most teachers want this for all their students, and they may need that regrounding—of this work—at times, we all need the reminder of our why. The following are some questions you can ask yourself as a facilitator of professional learning:

- Why is it important to integrate inclusive texts within all content areas?
- Why is it important for students to read outside of their bubbles?
- Why is it important for students to learn outside their bubbles?

An activity that is very powerful that helps to ground in purpose is the 5 Whys activity developed by Sakichi Toyoda, a Japanese inventor and industrialist. The 5 Whys activity is a root-cause analysis to find a solution to a problem and is a great tool to be able to find purpose in your professional learning. I suggest doing the 5 Whys activity anytime you provide professional learning to others.

Once you hone in on the purpose of professional learning, you must also be knowledgeable about the how. A question you can ask yourself is: How can you aid teachers in being able to integrate inclusive and diverse literature within varying content areas? Next, you must also think about what I am going to give teachers, especially in terms of resources and accessibility to these texts, for them to be able to integrate inclusive literature within varying content areas and lessons in seamless ways. All these questions asked are grounded in intentional curiosity and purpose. The bottom line is that teachers need to know the purpose, the impact, and the action they need to take. They also need to know how it is beneficial for them and their students. It is going to be important for teachers to know that this level of professional learning is important for their students' sense of self, their value, and their growth.

Planning for Professional Learning

We have taken time to get grounded in why we are facilitating this professional learning. Take time to think about your own beliefs behind providing and teaching with inclusive texts in classrooms.

Plan for the Purpose—The Why

We know ultimately our students are our *why* and the core of what we do— however, we also want to ensure that our teachers have the desire and belief to absorb this learning and can begin to take actionable steps to provide the most impactful learning experiences for all students. We want to ensure that through this professional learning, we are aiding in transforming learning and education so students are learning beyond the four walls of the classroom. We want our students to not only be good readers of text but able to think, read, write, and discuss past their bubbles and expand into the bubbles of others—that expansion of their bubbles is what can cultivate transformation. Once we are grounded in the why, and the purpose, we must take time to intentionally plan for the why of others. We can take time to make an intentional plan for that so we can answer when asked "Why are we doing this?" Be able to articulate well the purpose of professional learning around inclusive texts. Adults want to know the why and deserve to know the why, and we need to be ready to share that with them.

Plan for Connection Building/Create a Safe Space

Transformation begins from within. Take time within your sessions for teachers to connect around the purpose of meeting and the purpose of learning. It is also important to begin with time to connect before the actual learning takes place. Many times, as an instructional coach, I offered professional learning. There was one time in my beginning years as a coach when I wanted to offer an invitation to connect with the teachers before I began the learning session. The professional learning was centered around the book *The Best Part of Me* by Wendy Ewald.

I used the book to help the teachers connect to who they were as a teacher and their why. At first, I could feel their skepticism; however, as I continued, I saw some of their faces soften. I began by reading a few of the poems from the book where students celebrated parts of themselves and stated the reason it was their best part of them. I then had teachers think through a part of themselves as educators that was the best part of them and had them share why. Although the teachers I was coaching taught various subject areas, they all came together, shared, and connected through this prompt. They ended up loving it. They laughed and some cried; however, they felt safe enough to do so. They all were engrossed in literacy through poetry, they dug deeper into their identities, and they connected around the idea of threading themselves in a quick literacy connection that centered who they were at the core. It was a "feel good" connection moment, and the teachers were then ready to engage more and learn about what integrating texts, specifically inclusive texts, could look like for their students. Figure 9.1 shows a picture of the finished product of The Best Part of Me: Teacher's Edition.

Connection is the key to professional learning. When you offer that to teachers truly and authentically, you can open the doors to learning and relationships.

Plan to Dispel Possible Hesitancies

After connecting with teachers and helping them connect to each other, share what the learning is about. Take time to provide space for teachers to share how they may be already integrating inclusive texts in content areas—even in small ways. Have them think about the last inclusive book that they used in a lesson.

Figure 9.1   The Best Part of Me: Teacher's Edition

This will allow teachers to tap into prior knowledge and see that they may be already doing some of what they are learning about. If some are not already doing this work, teachers who are using inclusive texts in their lessons will usually take time to share an overview of their lessons, including how they used inclusive books in their lessons. Having an initial conversation surrounding the topic for learning can break down walls that may have been built to cultivate the opening of minds. This process helps teachers not only learn from the facilitator but also from each other.

Also discuss the possibility of a sense of hesitancy around using inclusive texts in their lessons and around integrating diverse books within various content areas. Before teachers begin to share, share with them at least three reasons why they might be hesitant to learn and engage in this professional learning. Take time to dispel the hesitancies—or the possibility of hesitancy. The first area of hesitancy may be that they are overwhelmed and have a lot on their plates. Teachers may feel as though they may not have the capacity to learn one more thing.

The second area of hesitancy, which may also be true, could be that they don't know how to even begin to put this impactful work into action. There may be fear of getting it wrong as they begin to integrate these inclusive texts into their lessons. They may even fear students not being receptive to the lessons. Another area of hesitancy may be that they just don't want to be there—that other things on their to-do lists must get done. This may be true, and as the facilitator of learning, try not to take it personally. Stating these possible hesitations may resonate with some teachers and not with others, but it allows the teachers to feel heard, seen, or even validated by the fact that you took time to think through areas that may cause hesitation in their learning.

Often, it is not the fact that teachers don't want to include diverse books in their lessons. They could be feeling overwhelmed or fearful, which may be causing hesitation. Taking the time to acknowledge, process, and discuss these emotions could help to release emotions, and bring them to the forefront so that you can build trust and the psychological safety needed for learning to move forward. Without having these important, maybe even uncomfortable, conversations, the essence of creating a psychologically safe environment and nonjudgmental zone is lost. When that is lost, it makes the time spent providing professional learning more challenging because you are only engaging in surface-level professional learning that won't lead to change. True professional learning that ignites change and gets at the core is professional learning that sustains.

Plan to Provide Research

Before providing professional learning, I urge you to take time to research how integrating inclusive texts across the curriculum increases student engagement and learning. This will help all of you, the facilitator and the learner, to ground even further into purpose and impact. Most teachers want to know the research behind the work they do, so take time to provide research at the onset.

One of many organizations that does this work is the nonprofit First Book, an organization dedicated to ensuring children, regardless of their background or ZIP code, can succeed by removing barriers to equitable education. Part of the work they do is getting inclusive books into the hands of students all over the country. First Book Research & Insights, the dedicated research arm of the nonprofit First Book, conducted a nationwide study to understand

- The importance of diverse classroom libraries from the educator's perspective
- The importance of diverse classroom libraries with respect to student outcomes

Through this intervention study, participating educators selected and added diverse books to their classroom libraries and completed bi-monthly tracking surveys to gauge the impact of those diverse books. The pilot study revealed that increasing access to diverse books in the classroom environment increases the amount of time that children spend reading and positively impacts students' reading scores (First Book, 2023). This study provided the access needed to the diverse literature for students. Students were able to have access to and read books with mirrors, windows, and sliding-glass doors. That alone impacted their reading engagement as well as their reading scores.

In another study, according to "Integrating Literacy Instruction with Science and Social Studies," researcher Timothy Shanahan states that the use of *content texts* (informational texts aligned to specific content areas) in reading comprehension lessons can improve content knowledge and reading ability. Teaching students how to use reading and writing in content classrooms can also have dual effects, and curriculum integration can have positive outcomes across a wide range of grades and with a wide range of students, including demographics and learning abilities (Shanahan, 2022). One could also conclude from this research that including diverse books, offering a variety of perspectives, and providing representation of the students being served and of students who may not be represented in the classroom can only increase engagement that much more. Taking the time to ground in purpose and including research to provide impact on the overall purpose by adding inclusive texts not only on the bookshelves in classrooms but in the lessons can further aid in taking actionable steps to do something different in teaching—doing something different in the professional learning provided to foster the change as well.

Plan for the Execution

The way that you execute professional learning matters. You want to plan professional learning around adult learning theory, which was first popularized by educator Malcolm Knowles in the 1980s. He popularized the concept of andragogy, the practice of teaching adults, and contrasted it with pedagogy, the practice of teaching children. Here are 10 simple principles of adult learning listed for future facilitators of professional learning to keep in mind as you engage in professional learning. When you plan for the execution of the learning, make sure to keep the following in mind:

1. **Adults Are Self-Directing:** For many adults, self-directed learning happens naturally without anyone explaining it or suggesting it. Adult learners are more prone to plan, carry out, and evaluate their learning experiences without the help of others. When instructing teachers, they need to set goals, determine their educational needs, and implement a plan to enhance their learning.

2. **Adults Learn by Doing:** Many adults prefer not only to read or hear about subjects but to actively participate in projects and to take actions related to their learning. The project-based curriculum utilizes real-world scenarios and creates projects for students that they could encounter in a job in the future. Many adult learners find that this kind of learning is hugely beneficial for them as they apply what they have been taught to their careers, giving them direct access to seeing what they can do with their knowledge.

3. **Adults Desire Relevance:** While some enjoy learning as an end in itself, adult learners are more likely to engage in learning that has direct relevance to their lives.

4. **Adults Utilize Experience:** Adults are shaped by their experiences, and the best learning comes from making sense of those experiences. Adult learners can greatly benefit from finding ways to get hands-on learning. Observing lessons, co-teaching opportunities, and other opportunities can help them get a firmer grasp of their learning and be more excited about how what they learn can be applied to their teaching.

5. **Adults Process with Their Senses:** Most adult learners don't thrive as well in a lecture-style environment. Due to the lack of brain plasticity in older learners, it's important to fully engage the senses when learning to successfully solidify new knowledge. Learning practices need to incorporate audio, visual, reading/writing, kinesthetic, independent, and group techniques.

6. **Adults Appreciate Repetition:** Repetition is essential for adult learning. If learners can practice new skills in a supportive environment, self-efficacy will develop to take those skills outside of the learning. And the more they can practice, the better the chances are for mastery.

7. **Adults Guide Their Own Development:** Utilizing dilemmas and situations to challenge an adult learner's assumptions and principles helps them guide their own development. Adults can use critical thinking and questioning to evaluate their underlying beliefs and assumptions and learn from what they realize about themselves in the process.

8. **Adults Thrive with Goal Setting:** Learners who have a specific teaching goal in mind will have a better experience as they learn. Adult learners need these goals because their learning is more in their own hands and they like having agency.

9. **Adults Learn Differently Than Children:** Children and adults are very different when it comes to how they learn, so different techniques must be used to make learning effective for adults. In addition to reading and

memorizing, adult learners utilize their past life experiences and their current understanding of professional learning as they learn.

10. **Adults Require Ownership:** With a more nuanced and advanced hierarchy of needs, adult learners place more value on intrinsic motivation and personal ownership of their learning. It's important to give adults internal motivation by recognizing their success and promoting increased self-esteem and confidence.

When executing your professional learning, it is key to keep these 10 principles of adult learning in mind (Pace, 2020) so your professional learning is followed through by the teachers in the learning community.

Integrating Inclusive Texts Professional Learning Pathways

Following professional learning pathways to ensure that teachers integrate inclusive texts in their lessons, we need to aid teachers in cultivating cultural competence and humility in their day-to-day work and in their lives. They need to take time to learn how to analyze diverse literature. Teachers need to also be taught how to teach strategies when using inclusive text. They need to review ways to evaluate student learning and to get the community involved in learning.

Cultivating Cultural Competence and Cultural Humility

We need to cultivate cultural competence and cultural humility. Cultural competence is a type of social fluency gained by learning about another culture's language, set of customs, beliefs, and patterns. Patterns of a culture are things that most do in certain situations within that culture. Being *culturally competent* helps educators to be responsive and sensitive to cultures. Cultural competence learning happens over time and on an ongoing basis. *Cultural humility* is an approach to sociocultural differences that is "self-first." It emphasizes intersectionality and understanding one's own implicit biases.

This approach cultivates self-awareness and self-reflection, bringing a respectful willingness to learn interpersonal interactions (Allaya Cooks-Campbell, Feb 2022). It means being grounded in curiosity, humility, courage, sensitivity, and love. This is a portion of the "L" step of the LEAP framework; however, when we move from individually learning and learning as a community, this training needs to occur.

Educators should undergo this learning to continue to deepen their understanding of diverse identities, experiences, and perspectives. This learning should cover topics such as relationship building, implicit bias, microaggressions, cultural sensitivity, and strategies for creating inclusive learning environments.

Inclusive Books Review/Analysis of Text

During professional learning, the facilitator should provide learning for educators to review and analyze diverse books. In the previous chapters, I discussed taking the time to vet books. I also included the necessary steps and resources to do so. Educators should take time to do this collaboratively in their teacher teams with a variety of diverse books to be able to choose high-quality inclusive and diverse books well and discuss ways to integrate them in lessons. Taking time to do this together allows folks to hear what makes the book high quality and what does not. Learning from one another is one of the most impactful ways to take in learning in meaningful ways and it helps to choose inclusive texts with intention.

Teaching Strategies and Curriculum Integration

Make the learning even more actionable and meaningful by taking the time to model a brief lesson for your teachers. The facilitator could also have teachers observe a teacher in action using inclusive texts in their classroom and observe the impact of having students read and learn outside of their bubbles. This observation time allows for teachers to see in action what it can look like, what it could sound like, and what strategies could be used, and then discuss the benefits of including diverse texts in their lessons. These discussions often allow teachers to ask questions to dig into the process of planning: aligning the diverse texts to learning standards, facilitating discussions, and cultivating engagement in the learning as well. This process makes professional learning impactful because teachers are learning from one another and not only the facilitator. After taking the time to observe, ask questions and discuss why it is important for teachers to have time to create. It is essential to provide space and time for them to create a lesson in their content area and intentionally integrate inclusive books within that lesson.

The best part about this process allows teachers to collaborate, share while creating, and even talk through any questions that arise. After they begin doing this, most likely they won't finish their lesson, but teachers can give feedback to one another and leave with lessons to teach their students—even if it is just in the beginning stages. Providing spaciousness for collaboration and discussion is most important. The discussion and collaboration fall on one of the higher steps of the learning ladder. Even though some educators may not complete the lesson within one session, providing time for teachers to work together will be pertinent to the learning and growth of the teachers. Completion is not necessarily the goal. The learning is in the doing, and the learning can be in the collaboration of a professional learning community—discussing, collaborating, learning, and understanding. A process like this one can take place after trust has been established and in an environment where teachers feel safe enough to engage in this type of learning. Learning where they can be open, honest, and share their worries, their fears, and their hesitations and be able to name and move through the emotions to get to the important learning at hand.

Evaluation of Student Learning

Transformation in education calls for a reimagination of how we evaluate students. Evaluation and discussion around the evaluation of students should also be a part of professional learning. I lean on Shane Safir and Jamila Dugan in their impactful and ongoing work, *Street Data: A Next-Generation Model for Equity Pedagogy, and School Transformation*. Street data is the qualitative and experiential data that emerges at eye level and on the lower frequencies when we train our brains to discern it. The data is asset-based, building on the tenets of culturally responsive education by helping educators look for what's *right* in our students, schools, and communities instead of looking for what is wrong (Safir & Dugan, 2021).

There are different types of evaluations when thinking about student learning that is asset-based versus working in the area of deficit.

Some of the items to use in the evaluation process is the use of artifacts, such as student work, student discussions, and items created by human beings. Another item that could be evaluated when thinking of student work would be the use of stories and narratives such as journals, interviews, etc. When thinking about evaluating, take time to reimagine what that could look like. What matters at the core of the evaluation of the humans in your classrooms in reading outside their bubbles? What do you want to know about each student as a reader, a thinker, and a learner? You can imagine and discern what matters collaboratively with the other teachers and leaders during professional learning.

While we want to take time to assess/evaluate student learning and understanding of inclusive text, we also want to make sure we are doing so in equitable ways. We want to ensure that we evaluate our teaching. Professional learning is a good time to be able to think about evaluating students in this work differently in collaborative learning spaces. Remember that evaluations don't just stop with our students. As we are learning, be open to evaluating yourself critically to grow and get better at teaching outside your bubble using inclusive texts. The learning continues for all.

Community Involvement

When thinking about reading and teaching outside of your bubbles, it is paramount to open the doors of your classroom and your schools to the community and families. We want to ensure that as we are engaging in our professional learning and engaging students in this learning, we are taking time to engage the community and families as well. We want to connect and be partners with families to partner with and offer support, equity, and access to inclusive texts in the school as well as getting them into the community and homes as well. Providing learning to our families, ourselves, and our students helps to build the learning community as a whole and provides alignment in this work.

Take Time to Reflect on Professional Learning

As you conclude each of your professional learning sessions, plan time to allow teachers to reflect on how they are feeling, what is coming up for them, what questions are still at the forefront of their minds, and the next steps.

Teacher Reflection

A couple of questions you could plan to ask teachers could be, do they feel that they can begin to integrate inclusive literature in their content areas? How did the creation lesson go? Allow for the reflections to be had and just take time to listen and to take it in. Provide the spaciousness for the possibility of next steps and understand that everyone's next step may look different.

Remind yourself as the facilitator that some teachers you may provide this learning to may already be doing this naturally, which is great. They can help to lead this work, and they will be helpful when discussing and supporting other teachers. Other teachers may need more support and hopefully other teacher leaders will be ready and willing to begin working together to continue this work for student and student learning.

Self-Reflection after Professional Learning

Self-reflection as the facilitator of any professional learning is also extremely impactful. As the facilitator, take time to reflect on what went well during the learning, what you could do differently, and next steps. After every professional learning that I facilitate, I usually give myself 10–15 minutes of self-reflection time. Taking time right after facilitating learning to write down what went well and what changes need to be made will help you to reflect and make the necessary changes for the next learning session.

During your self-reflection, make sure that you also consider the feedback that was given for the learning. Try to take in the positive feedback just as much as you take in the feedback for growth. As humans, we can be hard on ourselves. Allow yourself the space for what went well during the professional learning. Take that in. Then begin to focus on the growth areas. Remember we all have growth areas. We wouldn't be human if we didn't.

Ask for Feedback

As the professional learning facilitator, take time to ask for feedback from teachers for each of your sessions. Just as we want the teachers to grow in their craft, we also want to grow as the facilitators of professional learning. To do so, we must ask for feedback. Authentic feedback makes us better. It allows us to see what teachers felt went well, and it helps us know what they need to feel supported. We can ask for feedback in a number of ways. It can look like a Google survey, direct feedback, or feedback conversations. No matter how we choose to receive feedback, as facilitators we need feedback to model growth and learning. We can create a culture of growth and learning and provide an environment where we all can thrive.

Continue the Professional Learning

For everyone to thrive in your learning community, it is going to be important to continue to create an environment for learning. Professional learning is ongoing and continuous. As the facilitator or professional learning leader, take time to reach out to teachers who are integrating inclusive texts in their content areas or ones who want to begin this work, with your support alongside them. Support may look like coaching conversations, observations, co-planning, more one-on-one learning, feedback, etc. This is where you take the professional learning to even more action. This is ultimately where we want our professional learning to live—in the actionable spaces to see change. We want teachers to be able to begin implementation of the learning. We want them to feel confident to be able to implement the integration of inclusive texts in their teaching. We want them to feel comfortable enough to reach out if they need more support.

This is how a learning community is cultivated. We want a community that is centered on learning, rooted in our purpose, and doing what is in the best interest of all our students. We want our students to flourish and thrive in their learning environments, and we want our teachers to thrive while integrating inclusive text in content areas. We want students to read and learn outside of their bubbles. We want our teachers to also thrive in their learning and take their learning into action to ensure that students thrive. This is where we see change and transformation.

Let's Reflect

1. As a facilitator of professional learning, what do you feel will be a challenge as you plan and execute the professional learning? What steps can you take to overcome the challenges?

2. Planning for professional learning takes time. Take time to reflect and plan for your professional learning as it relates to your learning community.

3. Take time to review Knowles' adult learning principles as you plan for professional learning. Think about which of these principles are new to you as a facilitator of adult learning.

4. What comes up for you as you read this chapter? Take time to write.

Chapter 10
Banned Books = VIBs (Very Important Books)

Banned?

Banned books have always been society's way of hiding truth, silencing voices, and minimizing impact in our society. I remember in high school when *Romeo and Juliet* had the possibility of being banned—not that I was mad. But the fact that banning was being discussed intrigued me and angered me, even as a high school student. It made me want to read it even more. It was the thrill of finding out what could be written in that text to have it banned. I decided to read it on my own because curiosity got the best of me. However, I was assigned the text to read in class the following year as well. After reading it, I wondered what the drama was. The play wasn't even that good! Sorry/not sorry, Shakespeare. With all that, I was confused as to why *Romeo and Juliet* was subject to banning in the first place. But seriously, in high school 30 years ago, we talked about more sexual content in the school lunchroom than what that play discussed. Sadly, even today, a Florida school district is allowing students to read only excerpts of *Romeo and Juliet*, which do not include any sexual content. Again.

There are many school districts and school boards all over who are still banning books and attempting to ban books, even though students can easily find more sexual content on the Internet than in a 400-year-old tragedy.

In some instances, the students, teachers, and/or parents/caregivers have no idea that book banning is happening, but that isn't stopping some districts and leaders. It should come as no surprise that the books being targeted are ones with topics and titles about LGBTQIA+ characters, sexual orientation and content, race, racism, and books that have BIPOC characters as protagonists. In some states, books that are being banned are ones written by Black authors and authors of color. Book bans are directly related to the attempt to silence voices and bury accurate history.

Sadly, book bans have increased even more now than they ever have in previous years. The American Library Association reports the highest number of challenged book titles ever in 2023, with 4,240 titles being challenged by parents, community members, or decisions made by districts. That number truly is frightening. In 2023, the number of titles targeted for censorship at public libraries increased by 92% over the previous year, and school libraries saw an 11% increase. The titles that continue to be targeted represent the voices and lived experiences of LGBTQIA+ and BIPOC individuals. Emily Drabinski, the president of the American Library Association from 2023 to 2024, stated, "Every challenge to a library book is an attack on our freedom to read. The books being targeted again focus on LGBTQIA+ and people of color. Our communities and our country are stronger because of diversity. Libraries that reflect their communities' diversity promote learning and empathy that some people want to hide or eliminate." The truth is you cannot hide or eliminate history. A person can try—which is happening right now; however, there will always be someone willing to get in the fight. The fight for the freedom to read and learn from inclusive and diverse literature.

As an educator, the banning of books is a thorn in my side as I continue to do this work to ensure that students are reading outside of their bubbles. Even with the thorn, I continue to be a curious and open learner myself. However, when I see yet another book listed on a banned book list, I get filled with emotion and cannot believe that we are still fighting this same fight 30 years later. The task of fighting can become overwhelming, and I can only imagine how the authors, illustrators, and publishers of the books being placed on these lists may feel. I am only sure that it can feel disheartening, sad, and infuriating. I can only imagine the frustration they feel in trying to do their work and getting their books out into the world and then they being banned.

Authors of books on banned books lists—I salute you. I salute you for the work you put into getting your name noticed, writing your books, and getting them out into the world. Your books are important. Your books are needed. That is why I have invited a reframe into the mix as we continue to fight against the banning of books.

A Reframe: VIBs (Very Important Books)

What has helped me in my work of continuing to fight for the voices that are being silenced is a reframe I took on a while ago. The reframe helps me to look at banned books in another way and hopefully allows an illumination upon those books. The reframe is VIBs—Very Important Books. I began to look at banned books as ones that are in the VIB section of the library. I almost imagine it like when you go to a big event like a Beyoncé concert. I love Bey. When I go to a Beyoncé concert, it is usually sold out. There are different sections, just like there are a variety of sections in a library or bookstore. Some sections are a bit higher to the ceiling—the nosebleed section. Those are the books that everyone reads, like books that may have animal characters in them. Other sections in the concert venue are a bit closer to the stage, but Beyoncé is still a fair amount of space away from you. These are books that have thought-provoking or even "harder-to-handle" themes, but the characters are white. But then there is one section, a special section, the section that most want to be in. The section where you don't just get to see Beyoncé—you get to SEE Yoncé. You can see Beyoncé up close—her whole human self. This is the very important person, or what we would call the VIP, section. In the case of the banned books, it would be the VIB section. The section has books that are written by Black and Brown authors with Black and Brown characters or that have LGBTQIA+ characters. That has been my reframe. That's what banned book lists are to me. Banned books are in the VIB section of every library and/or bookstore.

Reading banned books is the section that you need to be in to see—up close—what the hype is about. The hype behind the ban. The hype within the book. What we come to realize as we read and immerse ourselves in the banned books is that this is the section that reveals truth, other perspectives, other voices, other lives, and authentic history. The truth is that banned books are where a good portion of reading and learning outside your bubble lives. Once you realize just how important banned books are, take inventory of which books are banned, the reading of these books increases, your knowledge increases, and your critical thinking increases. As teachers, this happens as well. Teachers, we need to do this work for ourselves and alongside our students for us to create the learning communities that foster not just students, but the community reading outside their bubbles. The learning space is where this needs to happen.

As students read outside their bubbles, they can also read about the injustices that have happened in the past and that continue to happen today. Students need spaces to name and critique injustice to help them ultimately develop agency to build a better world (Muhammad, 2020). The learning communities where reading outside of our bubbles and expanding the world are cultivated are where we can ultimately begin doing better. The more you know, the more you should want to know. The more you know, the more you want to do better. Doing better is where you become more actionable in your work and where you speak out to teach others. This is also a part of the learning ladder for inclusivity. This is when you, as the reader of banned books sitting in the VIB section, should speak up for everyone to be able to not just notice the banned books but to experience the banned books. This is where you move from mirrors and windows to sliding-glass doors and action. Books are under attack. More specifically, books that center those who are marginalized are under attack. It is time to speak up, advocate, experience, and learn from the books that are being placed on these banned books lists and share those books with others. These are very important books—the VIBs—that we need on our shelves and the ones that need to be utilized in our learning communities.

Using Our Voices

Who holds the power as it relates to the freedom to read? Isn't that a question that you ponder when you see a book placed on a banned book list? Who is using their voice to get these books placed on these lists? Where are the voices fighting against these book bans? Putting a stop to the banning of books requires one to think outside the box and tap into the courage within. This path highlights what is important; the important path is your right to not only choose what you read outside of your bubble but also what you can read to students to cultivate critical thinking, empathy, compassion, and love—to truly help transform the world we live in. There are a few ways to teach with and around the banning of books as well as be a voice to stop the banning of books. Sometimes the idea of using your voice can be scary, especially when you see educators losing their jobs by speaking up and taking action. However, if we don't use our voices, then banning books will continue to happen. Using our voices and influence is some of the most impactful work you can do to fight off the banning of books. There are some different ways to use your voice.

Raise Awareness

One way that you can do something and take action is by raising awareness. As I said earlier, oftentimes, the banning of books is happening under the noses of stakeholders. It is important to use your voice to raise awareness to let people know about the dangerous consequences of book bans. Using your voice does make waves. In the summer of 2024, a rural county in Texas reinstated eight books to its library, according to an appeals court. These eight books that addressed racism and LGBTQIA+ issues were ordered to go back on the shelves and be made available for checkout. Although these eight books are half of the number of books taken off the shelves, this is a step in the right direction.

Just as the librarian did in this Texas county, take time to use your voice. Use your voice to speak up on social media platforms, in your schools, at school board meetings, and in your school districts. Take time to use your voice to push for policies that oppose book bans, and advocate for inclusive texts to be used in your schools and integrated within the curriculum. When you hear your librarian at your school talking about the dangers of book bans, get on board and support them. Don't let them go at it alone. Remember, community is at the center. If you are not hearing the school or your community having these conversations, be the voice to start the conversation. Take time to ask questions and learn more. You can continue to encourage school librarians and local community librarians to purchase diverse and inclusive books for the library and for educator use. Lastly, use your voice to celebrate banned books and celebrate the freedom to read, discuss, and think critically about books that center marginalized groups. Raising awareness is important, and using your voice is one of the most powerful tools you can utilize.

Teaching Today with Book Bans Swirling Around

I would be remiss if I said that teaching today with book bans swirling around doesn't provoke fear. No one wants to lose their jobs. We have responsibilities and possibly families to support. I can understand that fear can creep up. However, in the state of this country, we must be able to teach truth without fear. We must do what we need to do to ensure that we teach our children to be changemakers in the society. We must lead them up the learning ladder. However, we must know our rights and policies in the state in which we reside to ensure our protection.

What Do the Policies Say?

In the state of Georgia, there was a 10-year veteran teacher who got fired from an elementary school after reading *My Shadow Is Purple* to her fifth-grade class, a book about being who you are, inclusivity, and gender fluidity by presenting a deviation from the traditional gender norms of associating blue with masculinity and pink with femininity. The teacher and the Teacher Association sued the district and its leaders. However, since the firing of that teacher, the district in which she worked has since removed even more books that are deemed to be "sexually explicit" from its library. Even in that county, there is a debate about who has the power in the district to make those decisions. However, in the age of book bans, whether we agree or not, it is going to be crucial that you as the educator take time to get to know the policies and procedures in your areas related to how schools or the school district selects books. You will also need to know what the procedure in your district is when a book is challenged. Find out what steps are taken when a book is challenged and when and if there is a possibility of a book ban. What is the process when that happens? Know the policies. Keeping up with policies and policy changes will be pertinent as you're teaching. As an educator, it is critical that you know that teaching is political, and because it is, you must know your rights and what to do if your rights are violated.

Teaching in Action: Know the Context

As you teach using books outside of your students' bubbles, first make sure that in each book you teach with or share you are providing historical and cultural context. You need to know the context when you share books with your students. Knowing the context lies in the "L" portion of the LEAP framework—starting with learning for self and moving toward teaching your students so they can also be aware of the historical and cultural context of the texts they are reading and learning from. As I stated in previous chapters, we want to make sure we are intentionally including books in our teaching. Being intentional means you have taken the time to vet the text using the questions and images I offered earlier in this book. Being intentional means you are thinking through how the text you are using or going to use aligns with the standard of learning that you are teaching your students. Intentionality in this area means that you are teaching and integrating multiple perspectives in your lessons by using the texts you have chosen. Intentionality also means that we are taking the time not only to read the book but also to know for ourselves the context of the books we read and teach to our students. One of many obligations of an educator is to make sure that we also know the context of the books that integrate into the lessons that we teach our students. That does not mean we don't use the texts and align them to standards, but knowing the context prepares us for questions and allows us to teach with the same intentionality that we used to plan.

Discuss the Why

Knowing the context of the book is important and important to teach students; however, as you begin using or use books that have been placed on the banned books or VIB list, I would take time to also have the students discuss why they believe that particular/specific book was banned. Encourage your students to take time to discuss critically what could have led to the censorship. Provide space for healthy discourse to happen. You want to make sure that all students feel psychologically safe throughout these discussions. In the previous chapter, I discussed having norms or agreements when discourse is occurring in the classroom. Remember norms and/or agreements allow for students to have parameters in how the discussions flow. It will be important for you to ensure that the students review the norms/agreements each time these discussions take place. This may sound redundant; however, the purpose of the norms/agreements is to try to ensure that your students aren't harmed during the discussions and discourse. We want everyone throughout the discussion to feel respected and heard. When we teach students, teach the context as you read and teach using inclusive books; allowing students to think critically about the text helps students to take in the learning. We want students to know that just because a book may have ended up on the banned books list does not mean that the book lacks value. We want students to be able to read topics, stories, and history from varying perspectives while being able to use their discernment of the why behind book bans. By students using their critical skills, we are allowing students to think for themselves and offer their thoughts as they read outside their bubbles. I offer more about reading critically in earlier chapters; if you want to dig in more, return to those chapters.

Be Prepared to Provide Options

Make sure as you teach using inclusive texts to also be prepared to give other options in texts that share the same viewpoint or perspectives. Be prepared to give other options for the inclusive texts you teach. An example of this would be if you are teaching your students about the civil rights movement. You have integrated the text written by Dr. Martin Luther King Jr.'s *Letter from Birmingham Jail* to your students during a lesson. However, it is helpful to provide options.

These options allow students to do comparative studies of varying texts with similar themes. You can then offer another text from that period written by Dr. Martin Luther King Jr. entitled "I've Been to the Mountaintop." The theme that threads these two texts together is injustice. That is one example of being prepared to provide options for your students to read and learn from as you navigate varying perspectives, texts, and illuminating voices during a lesson like the civil rights movement. Providing options in the texts you teach gives you the flexibility to change texts if that is needed as you navigate teaching your lessons.

Communicate with Caregivers and Families

With book bans swirling around, it will also help to communicate with families about the books being used in the classroom. Communication will always be key in teaching. This communication can happen at the beginning of the year, as well as throughout the year. In this communication, it will be important to make sure you let parents know that you will be including inclusive texts throughout the lessons that you will be teaching students. It is important in this communication that you take time to illuminate the positive factors and value of using diverse and inclusive texts in all classrooms. Share the level of increased engagement and love of literacy you have seen in your classroom when students read and learn from inclusive texts. It won't hurt to include research in your communication with families as well. I am including a sample letter here to send to parents as you embark on a new year (but you can edit and send this letter at any time of the year).

EXAMPLE LETTER TO PARENTS

Dear Parents/Guardians,

As we embark on a new academic year, I wanted to take a moment to share with you my approach to incorporating diverse literature into our classroom lessons and why I believe it is critically important for our students' education and growth.

In our classroom, we are committed to creating an inclusive learning environment that celebrates the richness of our diverse world. One of the ways we achieve this is through the careful selection of literature that represents a wide range of voices, experiences, and perspectives. This includes works by authors from various backgrounds.

Why is it important to include diverse literature in our curriculum?

- **Representation Matters**: Reading books featuring diverse characters allows all students to see themselves reflected in the stories they read. It validates their identities and experiences and fosters a sense of belonging and self-worth. We call these *mirrors* in our classroom.
- **Cultural Awareness and Understanding**: Exposure to diverse literature helps students develop empathy and understanding for people who may be different from them. It broadens their perspectives, challenges stereotypes, and promotes cultural competence. We call these *windows* and *sliding-glass doors* in our classroom.
- **Critical Thinking and Perspective-Taking**: Engaging with diverse literature encourages students to think critically about societal issues and consider multiple viewpoints. It enhances their ability to analyze complex themes and navigate the complexities of the world around them.
- **To Be a Part of Our Diverse World**: In a diverse world, it is essential for students to develop the skills needed to thrive alongside others in our colorful world. Exposure to diverse literature prepares them to embrace diversity with respect, empathy, compassion, and open-mindedness.

Throughout the year, your child will have the opportunity to explore a wide range of texts that reflect the diversity of human experiences.

We will engage in meaningful discussions, activities, and reflections to deepen their understanding and appreciation of these works.

I invite you to join me in supporting this endeavor by encouraging your child to embrace the diverse perspectives presented in their reading assignments. If you have any questions or concerns about the literature we will be exploring in class, please don't hesitate to reach out to me. Your feedback and involvement are invaluable as we work together to create a positive and inclusive learning environment for all students.

Thank you for your continued partnership in your child's education.

Warm regards,
Your Name

This letter is one you can use and modify to initiate communication about the learning that is happening within the classroom. By communicating with parents/caregivers, you offer transparency and openness to build trust with families. Family partnerships will be key to the success of their child throughout the school year.

I have named some strategies that you can implement as you navigate teaching amid book bans. Even though book bans are present, there are paths we can take to still give our students the impactful, important, and much-needed learning experiences they deserve inside and outside of the classroom. With parent/caregiver support, we can do so together. In partnership with parents, we can give students what they need at school and home. These inclusive learning experiences allow students to expand who they are, expand knowledge of themselves and others, and not only thrive as students in your classroom but as humans. When we can still give students the gift of reading outside their bubbles, they will be able to flourish. And we can still do that—even amid book bans. We can still read, learn, and teach outside of our bubbles. We can expand our world along with the worlds of our students—even with barriers that are being placed before us. We have always broken down these barriers. We still can.

What's Next with VIBs?

Book bans may continue to be an issue even after your advocacy, after using your voice, and after the work you do in your classroom every day. We must not lose heart. We must not forget our purpose. We must continue to advocate for the free-dom to read books inside and outside of our bubbles. It is up to educational lead-ers, teachers, and the family, like you and me, to continue to build, strengthen, and galvanize the community. Community is where our strength lives and will continue to live. We cannot do this work in silos. It is going to be important to not become weary in doing this work. It is also going to be important to lean on each other. Making sure that our very important books, our VIBs, are on the shelves and in the hands of students is critical work. It is work we must continue. We must continue to root in our purpose. We know the work we are leading and doing is for the betterment of us all—to expand our bookshelves, to expand our world, and to make our world better, one book at a time.

Let's Reflect

1. Do you know the policies as it relates to the banning of books in your learn-ing community? If not, take time to research and find out.

2. Have you taken the time to advocate for banned books or VIBs? If not, what is your hesitation? If so, what was the outcome?

3. Choose one of the strategies to take action and reflect on what that would look like.

4. What comes up for you as you read this chapter? Take time to write.

Epilogue

Read Outside Your Bubble is a title that I once thought would be changed or altered to be more "sophisticated" editing. I thought it would be changed to a title that others thought sounded super "intellectual" and more "prestigious." But the title did not change. The title was as it should be. Deep down, that is what I thought too. It is what I hoped. When I began using the #readoutsideyourbubble hashtag on social media to highlight the inclusive books that I post, I thought this is exactly what it means to read outside your bubble. It means to engulf yourself in inclusive books, read them, learn from them, and share them. *Read Outside Your Bubble* is much more than adding books to your shelves.

For me, reading outside my bubble was me getting super curious and having an open mind and open heart as I read outside my bubble. It is being a better listener to those around me and to what they were sharing—in the stories they were telling. Instead of listening to respond, I listened to them and read more to understand, not to just understand with my own eyes or ears but to get an understanding of life through the eyes of others. It is not being afraid to ask for clarity and more understanding when the relationship is established. For me, reading outside my bubble is not just adding books to my shelf but taking the time to digest them and truly take them in. When I read outside my bubble, I know that I must read and learn within my bubble as well. It is both. I can learn about myself and my walk in this life and learn about the walks of others. I can take the time to expand my reading into the paths of other folks in this world and find connections and differences. It is that ongoing learning for me that keeps me holding on to hope. I hope that maybe one day this world will be better at listening to one another and embracing each other. If I didn't do the things in this book and continue that work, I could not have written this book for you all and myself. I wanted a book that was able to capture the process of truly using inclusive texts in schools in ways that can cultivate change.

Reading outside your bubble, the hashtag, was one that I used to get folks to understand the importance of what this is—it is really being human. It is seeing the beauty in all people, cultures, races, and communities. This is the work of opening the eyes of others and of myself. It is the work of attempting to change the world. However, I wish it was that easy: to read a book and then—poof—one's eyes are open and the world is better. We are all on a journey of growth and learning. I read a lot. I learn a lot. And I have so much more learning and growing to do.

I wish I had all the answers to the problems of this world and the problems in education. I wish it was as simple as reading a book and all of the answers lie within it. But it isn't. In this book you have just read, I am sharing what I know and what I have learned from others doing this work. I believe in honoring the work of others who have gone before me. And one day maybe someone else will honor this work because I have gone before them. One thing I do know is that reading outside your bubble and teaching students to do so in inclusive, intentional ways can only increase the likelihood that your students are seen in the books on your shelves, that they feel valued, and that the work you do is not in vain. It is possible that the work of reading and learning outside of one's bubble may cause discomfort at times or may give birth to uncomfortable feelings. In that discomfort is often when the greatest learning is being born. Continue to do the work anyway.

We as educators are models in this work. We are often the ones holding the signs, leading the way in society toward change. We are the leaders in creating a just, compassionate, and loving world for us all. We do this work often without praise, acknowledgment, or even equitable pay. We do this work because we want to see a world that values, respects, cares, and empathizes with each other. We do this work because we believe in it and because we have hope that one day it will be different, where we don't have to write a book about the importance of reading outside your bubbles and expanding your world. I have hope that one day it will be different. Until then, we keep reading, learning, and teaching outside our bubbles because we know that it will change the world—our world. One book, one student, one teacher at a time.

References and Resources

10 Quick Ways to Analyze Children's Books for Racism and Sexism. https://wowlit .org/links/evaluating-global-literature/10-quick-ways-to-analyze-childrens-books-for-racism-and-sexism/

Audre, Lorde (1984). The Master's Tools Will Never Dismantle the Master's House. *Sister Outsider: Essays and Speeches*. Berkeley, CA: Crossing Press. 110–114.

Bell Hooks (2017, March 24). Building a Community of Love: bell hooks and Thich Nhat Hanh bell hooks meets with Thich Nhat Hanh to ask: how do we build a community of love? https://www.lionsroar.com/bell-hooks/

Bell Hooks (2000). *All About Love: New Visions*, Harper. New York: William Morrow.

Bettina L. Love (2023). *Punished for Dreaming: How School Reform Harms Black Children and How We Heal,* St. Martins Press.

Canadian Museum for Human Rights. https://humanrights.ca/story/us-vs-them-process-othering#:~:text=The%20process%20of%20othering%20can,mentality%20to%20alienate%20the%20group

Cooks-Campbell, Allaya. "Cultural Humility vs. Cultural Competence." *BetterUp*, 28 Feb. 2022, https://www.betterup.com/blog/cultural-humility-vs-cultural-competence.

Derald Wing Sue, Christina M. Capodilupo, Gina C. Torino, Jennifer M. Bucceri, Aisha M. B. Holder, Kevin L. Nadal, and Marta Esquilin (2007). Racial Microaggressions in Everyday Life: Implications for Clinical Practice. *American Psychologist*, 62, 4, 271–286

Duke, N. K., & Cartwright, K. B. (2021). The science of reading progresses: Communicating advances beyond the Simple View of Reading. *Reading Research Quarterly*, 56(S1), S25–S44. https://ila.onlinelibrary.wiley.com/doi/full/10.1002/rrq.411

Eesha Pendharkar Education Week. https://www.edweek.org/teaching-learning/book-bans-over-the-years-in-charts/2023/04

Elizabeth M. Ross. https://www.gse.harvard.edu/ideas/usable-knowledge/23/11/teaching-face-book-bans

First Book (2023). https://firstbook.org/wp-content/uploads/2023/09/2023-Impact-of-a-Diverse-Classroom-Library-FINAL-9-6-23.pdf

Gholdy Muhammad (2020). *Cultivating Genius*, Scholastic.

Gholdy Muhammad (2023). *Unearthing Joy*, Scholastic.

Gloria Ladson-Billings (2001). https://rethinkingschools.org/articles/teaching-and-cultural-competence/

Healthy Discourse Agreements. https://sheridan.brown.edu/resources/classroom-practices/discussions-seminars/sample-guidelines-classroom-discussion

Janet Taylor and Jed Dearybury (2021). *The Courageous Classroom: Creating a Culture of Safety for Students to Learn and Thrive,* Jossey Bass.

Jemima McEvoy, Sales Of 'White Fragility'—And Other Anti-Racism Books—Jumped Over 2000% After Protests Began. Forbes, July. 22, 2020. https://www.forbes.com/sites/jemimamcevoy/2020/07/22/sales-of-white-fragility-and-other-anti-racism-books-jumped-over-2000-after-protests-began/?utm_source=TWITTER&utm_medium=social&utm_content=3514900036&utm_campaign=sprinklrForbesMainTwitter#25105177303d

Kimi Pace, 10 Principles of Adult Learning. Western Governors University. April 7, 2020. https://www.wgu.edu/blog/adult-learning-theories-principles2004.html

Knowles, M. S. 1. (1980). *The modern practice of adult education: from pedagogy to andragogy.* Rev. and Updated. [Wilton, Conn.]: Chicago, Association Press.

Michael Creekmore and Nita Creekmore (2024). *Every Connection Matters*, ASCD.

Reading Diversity Tool. https://www.learningforjustice.org/sites/default/files/general/Reading%20Diversity%20Lite%E2%80%94Teacher%27s%20Edition2.pdf

Safir, S., & Dugan, J. (2021). *Street data: A next-generation model for equity, pedagogy, and school transformation.* Corwin.

Street Data: A Next-Generation Model for Equity Pedagogy, and School Transformation.

Timothy Shanahan (2022, April 18). Integrating Literacy Instruction with Science and Social Studies. Reading Rockets. https://www.readingrockets.org/blogs/shanahan-literacy/integrating-literacy-instruction-science-and-social-studies

Tracy Vasquez, Dusty Sanchez, and Alicia Kozimor (2021, October 5). Teaching & School Administration. https://www.gcu.edu/blog/teaching-school-administration/teaching-tuesday-literacy-content-area-instruction

Zaretta Hammond (2015). *Culturally Responsive Teaching & The Brain,* Corwin.

About the Author

Nita (E'Manita) Creekmore is an experienced teacher, instructional coach consultant, and presenter based just outside of Atlanta, Georgia, with more than 21 years dedicated to public education. Originally from Woodbridge, Virginia, Nita's career began in the classroom, where she spent 13 years teaching elementary grades before transitioning to a school-based instructional coach role for seven years. She also served as a presenter and coach for Bright Morning Consulting, where she worked alongside educators to drive meaningful change in teaching and learning practices for leaders and instructional coaches.

Nita earned a bachelor's degree in English (2001) and a master's degree in elementary education (2002) from the University of South Carolina. In 2013, she earned an educational specialist degree in educational leadership from the University of Virginia. Over the years, Nita has built a career grounded in her belief that relationships are the foundation of effective education—relationships with students, teachers, and the broader school community.

Passionate about advocating for both teachers and students, Nita serves as a thought partner and support system for educators, helping them provide the best possible learning experiences. She is particularly dedicated to integrating inclusive texts into educational spaces and curriculum to ensure diverse voices are heard and valued.

In addition to her work in education, Nita is the founder of Love. Teach. Bless, LLC, which is a space for educators grounded in the work of transforming education. She is also the co-founder of Creekmore Conversations with her husband, Michael Creekmore, Jr. Together, they co-authored *Every Connection Matters: How to Build, Maintain, and Restore Relationships Inside the Classroom and Out*, published by ASCD, a book that explores the power of relationship-building in education.

Outside of her professional work, Nita is committed to maintaining a healthy work–life balance. She enjoys spending time with her husband and four children—one son and three daughters—attending their extracurricular activities, practicing yoga, writing, resting, and unwinding with a good book. Nita firmly believes in the importance of self-care and personal well-being to sustain a meaningful life. Find out more about the work of Nita Creekmore at love-teach-bless.com.

Index

Note: Page references in *italics* refer to figures and tables.